THE
FIELD & STREAM

All-Terrain
Vehicle
Handbook

Books by Monte Burch

Denny Brauer's Jig Fishing Secrets
Denny Brauer's Winning Tournament Tactics
Black Bass Basics
Guide to Calling & Rattling Whitetail Bucks
Guide to Successful Turkey Calling
Guide to Calling & Decoying Waterfowl
Guide to Successful Predator Calling
Pocket Guide to Seasonal Largemouth Bass Patterns
Pocket Guide to Seasonal Walleye Tactics
Pocket Guide to Old Time Catfish Techniques
Pocket Guide to Field Dressing, Butchering & Cooking Deer
Pocket Guide to Bowhunting Whitetail Deer
Pocket Guide to Spring & Fall Turkey Hunting
Guide to Fishing, Hunting & Camping Truman
The Pro's Guide to Fishing Missouri Lakes
Waterfowling, A Sportsman's Handbook
Modern Waterfowl Hunting
Shotgunner's Guide
Gun Care and Repair
Outdoorsman's Fix-It Book
Outdoorsman's Workshop
Building and Equipping the Garden and Small Farm Workshop
Basic House Wiring
Complete Guide to Building Log Homes
Children's Toys and Furniture
64 Yard and Garden Projects You Can Build
How to Build 50 Classic Furniture Reproductions
Tile Indoors and Out
The Home Cabinetmaker
How to Build Small Barns & Outbuildings
Masonry & Concrete
Pole Building Projects
Building Small Barns, Sheds & Shelters
Home Canning & Preserving (with Joan Burch)
Building Mediterranean Furniture (with Jay Hedden)
Fireplaces (with Robert Jones)
The Homeowner's Complete Manual of Repair and Improvement (coauthor)
The Good Earth Almanac
Survival Handbook
Old-Time Recipes
Natural Gardening Handbook
Field Dressing and Butchering Rabbits, Squirrels, and Other Small Game
Field Dressing and Butchering Deer
Field Dressing and Butchering Big Game
Field Dressing and Butchering Upland Birds, Waterfowl, and Wild Turkeys

THE
FIELD & STREAM
All-Terrain Vehicle Handbook

**The Complete Guide to Owning and
Maintaining an ATV**

Monte Burch

The Lyons Press
Guilford, Connecticut
An imprint of The Globe Pequot Press

Copyright © 2007 by Monte Burch

Originally published in 2001 by The Lyons Press

Additional revised information copyright © 2007 by Monte Burch

The Lyons Press is an imprint of The Globe Pequot Press.

10 9 8 7 6 5 4 3 2 1

Printed in the United States of America

ISBN: 978-1-59228-888-5

The Library of Congress has previously cataloged an earlier (paperback) edition as follows:

Burch, Monte
    The Field and Stream all-terrain vehicle handbook: the complete guide to owning and maintaining an ATV / Monte Burch.
        p. cm.
    Includes bibliographical references.
        ISBN 1-58574-212-0 (pbk.)
        1. All terrain vehicles. I. Title: All-terrain vehicle handbook.
II. Field & Stream. III. Title.
    TL235.6.B85 2001
    629.22'042—dc21   200102987

Contents

Author's Note

The ATV market continues to grow rapidly as more and more out-door people discover the fun of their use, as well as the practicality. With lots of new products and ATVs on the market, especially in the utility vehicle market, we have decided to update and bring out this revised edition. At readers' request, we have included more actual tests of specific vehicles in this edition.

Acknowledgments

I would like to thank the many manufacturers who have supplied vehicles and products for testing and photographing, as well as for supplying photos and product information. I would also like to thank the various magazines and their editors who have allowed me to use material and photographs from my articles and columns in their magazines.

Introduction

At 11,000 feet the trail was mighty narrow, with a drop of hundreds of feet. Several thousand feet below, the silvery sparkle of a river snaked through the valley. It was an awesome sight, but my attention was riveted on the trail before me and my hands were in a death grip on the ATV handlebars. A short time later, and with dark clouds forming quickly, we reached our destination, a packers campground high in the Utah mountains. A sudden hailstorm made setting up camp a difficult task. But, typical of mountain country, the storm was over as fast as it came in and we were treated to a star-studded night. The next morning we continued our ride on the beautiful Paiute ATV trail in Utah and on to the Rocky Mountain ATV Jamboree in Richfield, Utah.

The river was up and forbidding, but crossing it was our only option. Steep mountains rose on both sides of the tiny valley, their sides covered with the verdant vegetation of Kodiak Island in Alaska. We eventually got everybody across without mishap only to discover the trail led through a deep muddy bog. Things got a little trickier then, but again we made it and continued on our destination to hunting camp.

The trail made a sharp dip, then an immediate turn to the right, another sharp drop, a creek crossing, then a 90-degree turn and up a boulder-strewn trail, some boulders marked with streaks of metal. The rider before me, an expert off-road racer, was well out of sight, but I kept my somewhat slower pace, enjoying the competition, and mostly challenging myself. The Chadwick ATV trail in the Ozarks was definitely challenging.

The ATV rumbled powerfully forward, the disc behind turning over the dark, loose soil. By noon I had the entire food plot tilled and planted, and glancing at my daughter Jodi's stand thought to last year's hunting success and wondered about the coming year.

At the crack of the rifle shot I grinned to myself. It came from the direction of Jodi's deer stand and she just doesn't miss. Within seconds another rifle shot, this time from the direction of my wife's stand. "Two down, I hope," I muttered to myself as I climbed down from my stand and headed for the house. A short time later Jodi and I were loading her fat doe onto the back of our ATV and headed for home. While Jodi began field dressing her deer, I headed for "Momma's" stand.

Loaded with hundreds of snow goose decoys, a husky Lab, my partner, and hunting gear, the Kawasaki Mule easily made it across the frozen ground to the pit blinds we had dug the evening before. With decoys set just before dawn, I motored back to hide the Mule and saw the beginning skeins coming off the lake. I just had time to get back to the blind.

"Do you think we can get this one stuck," said James Hall with a grin. We didn't, but it was great fun at the Guns & Gear Magazine ATV Shootout in Alabama. We spent a week testing seven of the top utility ATVs and seven utility vehicles from the major manufacturers. We ran them all through acceleration tests, food-plot plowing, measured for ground clearance and turning radius, and ran them up and down hills, over boulders, through mudholes, and water.

We discovered they were all great vehicles, each offering its own features. We also thoroughly enjoyed the fun of ATVing. That's what a large number of other folks are quickly discovering, too.

All the events described took place in about a year's time and reveal the fast-growing interest in ATVs. ATV sales continue to grow at an unprecedented rate. Part of this is due to the increased ability of manufacturers to produce more user-friendly vehicles—mainly in the automatic utility sector. Those models, used for everything from pleasure riding to farming, ranching, job-site chores, and especially hunting now make up well over a third of the total sales of ATVs.

Hunters and anglers in particular have become an increasingly growing market. If you hunt deer, waterfowl, upland game, own a hunt club or just like experiencing the outdoors, you can enjoy it all more with an ATV. Four seating utility vehicles have also become increasingly popular not only for toting a couple of buddies and gear to their hunting stands, but also for farming, ranching and even pleasure trail riding.

This book describes the ATVs available, their uses, safety, and riding techniques. It also describes the numerous accessories that make recreation and chores easier as well as places to ride for pleasure, and needed maintenance.

Here's to fun, safe riding, and I hope to see you on the trail.

CHAPTER 1

Understanding ATVs

All-terrain vehicles (ATVs) have gone from simple, three-wheeled fun machines to sophisticated models capable of handling a variety of chores and providing lots of fun as well. Numerous sizes, shapes, and models are available from a number of companies. Understanding the basic types is important in order to choose the best ATV for your purposes.

HISTORY OF ATVS

Three decades ago, no one could have predicted that Honda's fertile imagination and three fat tires would develop into a vital part of American fable and leisure—one that currently sells more than 400,000 units per year. But from the moment the original all-terrain vehicle (which Honda trademarked as the ATC)—Honda's US 90—debuted in 1970, that's exactly what happened.

If necessity was the mother of the first ATV, Honda engineer Osamu Takeuchi was its father. In 1967, American Honda asked Honda R & D, Ltd., for a new product that dealers could sell when motorcycle sales cooled off in winter. Takeuchi was assigned to lead the project, along with a small group of Honda engineers. This was clearly the group for the job, since Takeuchi and company had been working to develop other new recreational vehicles that never saw production. These projects gave Takeuchi the tools to develop Honda's US 90.

Forget the proverbial blank sheet of paper. Takeuchi started in the shop with a head full of ideas and an eclectic assortment of components. Two-, three-, four-, five-, and even six-wheeled configurations were examined, but the three-wheeled concept delivered the

All-terrain vehicles (ATVs) are steadily becoming an important part of today's outdoor recreation, as well as workhorses for farmers, ranchers, landowners, and many others. (Photo courtesy Yamaha)

best combination for the machine's intended mission. It handled snow, mud, and assorted slippery conditions a two-wheeler couldn't, while providing more maneuverability than other configurations.

In the early stages, a Honda ST70 motorcycle gave up its 70cc four-stroke single-cylinder engine for the cause, along with assorted chassis parts. An extended rear axle carried cultivator wheels designed to handle rough terrain. Two driving wheels in the rear worked well. Cultivator tires didn't. The biggest challenge was finding a tire capable of getting a grip on soft, changeable terrain such as snow, sand, and mud. Two wheels, three wheels, four wheels, or more? Motorcycle tires weren't an option.

The design process quickened when American Honda sent Takeuchi an American invention called the Amphi-Cat, which rolled on six 20-inch low-pressure, high-flotation balloon tires. The light-

ATVs began as three-wheel fun machines over three decades ago with the Honda US 90 ATC. (Photo courtesy Honda)

bulb went on. Revamping his ST70-based prototype to accept the new low-pressure rolling stock, Takeuchi went to work on his own tire design, settling on 22-inchers inflated to 2.2 psi. With the tire dilemma solved, Takeuchi discovered that the 70cc engine lacked the muscle necessary to push a full-sized rider through snow or mud. A 90cc engine running through a special dual-range four-speed gearbox added to the requisite flexibility over varied terrain.

The next phase of development was optimizing the chassis to match the new engine and tires. Testing over rough roads, sand hills, and slopes as steep as 35 degrees gradually established chassis dimensions effective for recreational riding as well as agricultural work. Laid out in the shape of an isosceles triangle with the foot pegs located outside the triangle to optimize control, the ATC design was unique enough to permit Takeuchi to patent the arrangement.

Exhaustive testing brought other lessons to light. Using a thumb throttle instead of the typical motorcycle twist grip let riders shift their weight for optimal vehicle maneuverability while maintaining precise throttle control. A rear differential was considered, but discarded when a live axle performed better. Though suspension is an integral part of the modern ATV, Takeuchi's original balloon tires soaked up rough terrain best by themselves.

Exerting less pressure on soft or sensitive terrain than the average human foot, these tires let the vehicle go places others couldn't, leaving little or no evidence of their passing—an advantage that looms large in hundreds of modern ATV applications.

Officially introduced in 1970, the US 90 sent its 7 horsepower through a dual-range, four-speed gearbox with an automatic clutch, and sold for $595. It was renamed the ATC90 later that year when Honda, as noted, trademarked the ATC brand. Three models carried the Honda ATC monogram through the 1970s. The ATC70 gave younger riders a scaled-down version of the fat-tire experience. By the end of the decade, requests for more power had turned the original ATC90 into the ATC110 in 1979. From the beginning, the ATC was as evolutionary as it was revolutionary.

Good as the original fat tires were on snow and sand, they were vulnerable to punctures from such things as the stubble from harvested crops. The fact that those original tires weren't repairable compounded the problem, so a fabric carcass was added, and steel hubs replaced the first hubless wheel design in 1975. Tougher, color-impregnated plastic fenders were also added in that year.

Though it was primarily a recreational vehicle through the 1970s, the ATC began to make inroads with farmers, who realized it was a tool that could make their lives easier. Honda engineers followed their machines into the field, gathering data to help the ATC adapt to a rapidly growing market. The ATC was as capable at labor as at leisure, and America was catching on.

Moving into the 1980s, two arenas looming large in the ATV world were utility and racing. The popularity of utility usage was easy to understand. On the farm, an ATV used 8 percent of the fuel consumed by a tractor, while the latter cost exponentially more to purchase and maintain. Consequently, utility usage exploded in the 1980s and ATVs became multipurpose machines, serving both recreational and utility purposes. In 1985, 70 percent of ATVs were used primarily for recreation; today, 80 percent see multiple uses.

Introduced in 1980, the ATC185 was popular among utility users. Rolling on larger, 25-inch tires that afforded improved traction, the 185 featured a five-speed transmission, an automatic clutch, and a 180cc four-stroke, single-cylinder engine that was considerably more powerful. Though designed to split its duties more or less equally between work and play, the 185 set the stage for Honda's first purpose-built ATV two years later.

The 1982 ATC200, aka Big Red, had more of everything necessary to get a host of jobs done. Its 192cc engine and five-speed, dual-range gearbox cranked out more power, especially low in the revolution band, to make chores such as towing, spraying, seeding, and fertilizing easier. Adding an electric starter to the standard recoil system made starting the day as easy as pushing a button. Dual racks and a 9.2-liter storage box made carrying tools, hay bales, fencing, and other agricultural essentials easier. A new sealed rear drum brake survived muddy fields and water crossings, and a telescopic fork front suspension made a day in the saddle much more comfortable. Big Red added a reverse gear in 1984, and its drive chain was replaced with a shift drive for extra durability and less maintenance.

The other major ATV theme of the 1980s—racing—was played out everywhere from frozen lakes in the East to western deserts to the dirt ovals of Middle America. Meanwhile, the utility ATV market was beginning to swing toward another wheel. Honda's first four-wheeled ATV, the TRX 200, debuted in 1984. Four-wheelers were considered more versatile tools by customers—and tools were what people wanted most. By 1985, the smart money in the ATV world was on four wheels.

Skyrocketing ATV sales inevitably led to an increase in accidents, prompting an investigation by the Consumer Product Safety Commission (CPSC). In 1986, CPSC statistics suggested that most ATV accidents were attributable to improper riding behavior that ignored the manufacturers' warnings. No inherent flaw was found in the three- or four-wheeled ATV design.

ATV manufacturers' manuals and product warning labels stressed the importance of proper vehicle operation to customers. A national industry safety campaign resulted in a 33 percent decline in injuries reported to the CPSC between 1984 and 1988. Regardless, on April 28, 1988, distributors in the United States entered into an unprecedented 10-year agreement with the CPSC called the "Final

Due to safety reasons, today's ATVs utilize four wheels instead of three. (Photo courtesy Arctic Cat)

Consent Decree." The ATV industry made a $100 million commitment to expand existing safety programs, while free training and training incentives were offered to current ATV owners and purchasers of new models. Additionally, distributors would no longer market three-wheeled ATVs, and would buy back any unsold three-wheelers from dealer inventory. Three-wheeled ATV sales were already trailing off, but the CPSC agreement did serve to accelerate the process.

Throughout the 1980s, more and more people saw the ATV as a vehicle capable of making thousands of different jobs easier and faster. By the 1990s, the four-wheeled ATV had become an essential part of the great American toolbox. These days you'd be hard pressed to find a Louisiana rice farm, Washington apple orchard, Montana cattle ranch, or hunting operation anywhere that doesn't have at least one.

ATV BUYERS

Five groups of ATV buyers have been identified by manufacturers. Casual recreationists are the "toy buyers"; their interests revolve around family fun, relaxation, and social interaction. This group, which comprises about a fifth of the market, contains a high percentage of first-time buyers, and they tend to be less experienced riders. This group also enjoys the highest household income of the five groups, has the highest percentage of white-collar occupations, and holds the highest share of female riders.

Outdoorsmen ATV owners have comprised about a quarter of the ATV market, although this segment is growing. Their favorite activities are hunting, fishing, and exploring. They buy ATVs primarily as a means to help them enjoy some other activity (such as hunting), or to get them to their favorite fishing spot. These owners are about in the middle of the income range, and three-quarters of them are married.

ATV buyers range from those who ride for pleasure to off-road racing to hunting. Hunters and agri-hunters, or those who hunt and own the land, are the fastest growing groups of buyers. (Photo courtesy Suzuki)

The agri-hunters are the fastest-growing group. They are most likely to buy an ATV for work purposes first, then use it for play. They're second only to the outdoorsmen in their interest in hunting, but are not involved in a wide range of recreational activities. This is the most mature and oldest segment among the five, almost all are married, and they have the second highest household income. Many agri-hunters own their own farms.

Perhaps the most interesting of the five groups is the passionate adventurer. These owners are deeply involved in the total experience of ATV riding. They ride to have fun, relax, and gain a sense of freedom. They are goal oriented in their ATV riding, and are the most likely to plan outings with their ATV as the focal point of their activities. They'll ride anywhere, anytime they can.

The last group encompasses the high performers, the performance enthusiasts of the ATV world. They make up one-fifth of the total market; they're into top-speed extreme handling and the excitement of riding. Riding is a very social activity for this group, and members tend to view their ATV as an extension of their personality. These users are competitive, and share a desire to be in control. They're the youngest of the five groups, averaging 28 years, and have the lowest incomes.

ATV TYPES

Three basic types of ATVs, not counting utility vehicles (which will be covered in a later chapter), have evolved to suit the needs of the five different rider groups. These are sport models, used by high performers and to some extent by casual recreationists; utility models, used for a wide range of work and recreation activities by all the groups except the high-performance riders; and the utility/cargo ATVs. The last type, which is the smallest segment, usually features a cargo box for hauling gear. They're the most popular with farmers, ranchers, and outfitters. A wide range of ATV sizes, price ranges, and features are available from the different manufacturers.

ATVs are available with kick starters, pull starters, and electric start. They may be water cooled or air cooled. Machines may have automatic clutches, hand-operated clutches, or fully automatic transmissions. Some have reverse gear. Models are available with

Sport model ATVs are designed and primarily used for off-road racing and pleasure riding. (Photo courtesy Suzuki)

solid-drive axles, and some have differentials. Two-wheel drive, four-wheel drive, and shift-on-the-fly between the two are also on the market. ATVs may have chain or shaft drives. A purchaser must consider what chores or pleasures the vehicle will be used for when choosing an ATV.

Sport Models

Sport-model ATVs are primarily used for recreational riding, off-road racing, and other speed sports. These models are quicker and more responsive than the utility models. Sport models are also available in several engine sizes, including models for youngsters.

Sizes range from under 50cc to well over 700cc. The majority of the sport models feature manual shifting, although the youngster models may have automatic or semiautomatic transmissions.

Sport models are available in a variety of engine sizes. (Photo courtesy Kawasaki)

Utility ATVs

Utility ATVs comprise the largest segment of vehicles, and are the main focus of this book. Although they are available with manual shift, especially in the lower-priced models, automatic shift has become increasingly popular, as has electric start. Engines range in size from around 200cc to well over 700cc. Utility models feature softer suspensions than the sport models, and are available in two-wheel drive, four-wheel drive, and models that can be switched between the two.

Two-wheel drive affords better performance on trails and at higher speeds. Four-wheel drive provides the traction needed for mud, extremely rough off-road work, and pulling implements, hauling out logs, and other chores. Switching between modes is fairly easy on most models. Some now come with automatic switching or four-wheel drive on command. These are the best of both worlds, but also the most costly. Some high-end models offer front differential lock, which adds even more traction in the tough spots. Most utility bikes are designed as workhorses, with large racks on both front and back to carry items. When purchasing a unit, check the rack capacity as well as the towing capacity.

Utility models make up the largest segment of ATVs. Designed for both work and pleasure, they are available in a wide range of engine sizes and configurations. (Photo courtesy Yamaha)

Utility models feature larger frames with racks on front and back to carry gear or other loads. (Photo courtesy Yamaha)

Electric start is a very popular feature of today's utility market.

Automatic transmissions are extremely popular on utility models, and one reason for the fast-growing popularity of utility models.

Utility models are available as two-wheel, four-wheel, and with the ability to shift between the two.

Engine braking has become an increasingly popular feature on the higher-end machines. This feature slows the vehicle when going downhill, rather than having the unit free-wheel, which requires you to apply the brakes. Engine braking provides a safer and more controllable ride. The amount of engine braking can vary a great deal among models and manufacturers.

Over the past few years, a number of innovations have developed, with independent rear suspension now offered on most manufacturers' top-end models. Many also offer a 2-inch receiver hitch. Lights and racks, fenders, brakes, and footrests have all been improved greatly. And some manufacturers offer ATVs capable of carrying two.

Following is a summary of some of the top utility models currently on the market and their main features, designed to give you an idea of what's out there. Some of the models have been added since the last printing of this book. Others have become classics and are still available. Each of the manufacturers also has numerous other models.

Kawasaki Brute Force 750 4x4i

The Kawasaki Brute Force 750 4x4i ATV is all about performance. Kawasaki introduced the ATV world to high-performance 4x4 utility ATVs with their Prairie 650 4x4 and its successor, the Prairie 700 4x4. Each machine has an awesome V-twin engine and great ride and handling.

Kawasaki tops its own success with the Brute Force 750 4x4i. I tested the ATV under several conditions. As you can guess, the engine power is awesome. From a dead stop, drop the throttle and power is instantaneous. Up in the midrange, you also have a lot of backup power for quick acceleration when needed. And on top, the machine can make your heart pound. Powering the Brute Force is Kawasaki's revolutionary 90-degree, four-stroke V-twin engine. With a bore and stroke of 85 x 66mm, it displaces 749cc and features new plated aluminum cylinders, a reverse-facing air intake, new 34mm downdraft carburetors and straight intake tracts, and four valves per cylinder.

One of the features I liked about both the previous Prairie models was the Kawasaki Engine Brake Control. This helps slow the vehicle when traversing steep downhills. Some of the trails I tested the new 750 on had quite challenging dips and turns, and the 750 engine braking was extremely good, providing instant braking response with throttle let-off. Another feature I appreciate is the high-efficiency radiator mounted high in the chassis. This protects the machine from mud and debris and also from obstacles poking into it.

Like the Prairie 700, the 750 transfers power from its V-twin engine to the wheels through a continuously variable transmission (CVT) featuring high and low ranges, plus reverse. By simply pressing a button on the handlebar, you can select two- or four-wheel drive. In four-wheel-drive mode, the Brute Force utilizes a limited-slip front differential. This provides easier steering under most ground conditions. When you really need traction, however, you can pull the lever on the left-hand handlebar and engage the Variable Front Differential Control, which delivers torque equally to the right and left front wheels.

The front driveshafts of the Brute Force feature Cardan joints—another industry first. Similar to U-joints, Cardan joints help absorb torque fluctuations to the driveshaft. The lightweight design helps to reduce vibration.

Another great feature is the new fully independent rear suspension (IRS) system. The 750 is the first Kawasaki 4x4 to feature this type of suspension. An independent rear suspension allows for much more flexibility at the rear end and more maneuverability. You can literally crawl over boulders, logs, and other obstacles. And the riding balance is much better as the suspension adjusts to the terrain. The rear final gear case and sealed rear braking system have been redesigned in conjunction with the new IRS. Smaller and more compact, the gear case is nevertheless extremely rugged and efficient.

Actually, the first thing you'll notice about the Brute Force is the seating position. You sit more upright and nearly 2.5 inches higher than on the Prairie 700. At first I thought this might cause handling problems on sharp turns, but not so. In fact, I was better able to shift my body weight in the new position, which provides a better view of the terrain, too. The seat has been redesigned with more padding for better comfort. The new automotive-style instrument panel is positioned more vertically to suit the changed riding position.

Dual front disc brakes and Kawasaki's distinctive sealed rear braking system provide plenty of stopping power. The rear system is completely sealed to protect against mud, dust, and debris. The vehicle's compact size also provides for more ground clearance than a conventional rear disc brake system.

Kawasaki Prairie 650 features the industry's first V-twin engine, a huge 633 model. Model is two- or four-wheel drive selectable with a switch. (Photo courtesy Kawasaki)

The Brute Force 750 4x4i has a simple yet sturdy double-cradle frame made of tubular steel, while the suspension is all new for a Kawasaki 4x4 ATV. Rather than the MacPherson struts and aluminum swingarm featured on the Prairie 700 4x4, the Brute Force features front dual A-arms and the IRS rear system. The front dual A-arms have adjustable shocks with 6.7 inches of travel, while the IRS features a leading torsion bar and provides 7.9 inches of travel. By utilizing a combination of needle bearings and ball joints in the lower rear A-arms, the IRS provides smoother suspension action for greater stability. This answered my first question about potential handling problems with the higher seating position. And this suspension offers great comfort, regardless of terrain. The combination of chassis and suspension provides the Brute Force with 10.6 inches of ground clearance—an inch more than that of the Prairie 700. In addition, the Brute Force rides on restyled wheels shod with 12-inch tires featuring larger, more aggressive tread blocks. The gas tank is located beneath the seat for better balance and handling.

Kawasaki is using the redesigned body of the Brute Force as the blueprint for future 4x4 ATVs. The front grille is bigger, stronger, and tougher looking than the Prairie lineup. Made of ThermoPlastic Olefin, a new plastic with a high-gloss appearance and that's scratch resistant. Available colors include Aztec Red, Hunter Green, Desert Yellow, and Realtree Hardwoods Green HD camouflage. One problem I encountered was that the front fender flares seemed a bit narrow, allowing mud and dirt on my pant leg during mud runs. Then again, these fenders aren't as likely to catch on brush as those with more aggressive flares.

Other features include the ATV industry's first four-bulb headlights, which provide a great swath of lighting for nighttime rides. Storage compartments located in the left and right front fenders offer gear storage. Like the Prairie 700 4x4, the Brute Force 750 4x4i features full-sized floorboards.

Polaris 500 H.O. RSE (Remington Special Edition)

The Polaris Sportsman 500 Remington Special Edition has become one of the most popular utility ATVs on the market. It was introduced in 1985, and Polaris produced the one millionth automatic model in 2001. In my tests, the Polaris 500 H.O. proved an excellent ATV, passing speed and pulling tests with flying colors. Part of the

Polaris 500 H.O. in the popular Remington Special Edition has powerful engine braking feature, on-demand four-wheel drive.

performance is attributable to a high-output engine, managed by the water-resistant Polaris dual-sensing sealed automatic transmission, with Polaris EBS (Engine Braking System). No shifting is required; the unit is fully automatic, with an E-Z Shift high and low gear range plus reverse. The dual-sensing transmission responds to both engine RPM and vehicle torque requirements to provide superior backshifting in all riding conditions. Polaris stands behind their transmission with a lifetime belt warranty. One of the main strengths of the 500 is its superior engine-braking performance. On long downhill runs, it produced very noticeable slowdowns quite rapidly. A skid plate on the bottom further protects the transmission.

Additional traction is provided instantly by the Polaris intelligent on-demand true four-wheel-drive system. This system senses when the rear wheels lose traction and automatically engages both front wheels, providing full torque to all wheels. Power is delivered by an independent driveshaft system. The automatic system is activated by pushing a thumb switch. With the unit in four-wheel drive, I was able to scoot up to logs, then climb up and over them quickly and easily.

The Polaris exclusive progressive-rate independent rear suspension with a pair of twin-tube shocks and a stabilizing antiroll bar also provides a unit with a rear dual arm, not straight, and an industry-leading ground clearance of 11 inches. Up front, the MacPherson strut independent suspension has 6.7 inches of travel (or bounce).

The single-lever, all-wheel hydraulic disc brakes have heat-treated discs and improved pads for longer life in all braking conditions. Stainless-steel braided brake lines provide great brake handle feel.

The Special Edition comes with front and rear rack extenders and front and rear tube bumpers, as well as the signature Remington Logo and Mossy Oak camo pattern. I've tested several of these models. The first I had for about a month, riding it hard in my deer woods. It came through without a scratch, even after bulldozing over saplings, brush, and briars to get to a prime deer stand site. Another feature I like is the adjustable high-mounted quartz halogen headlight in the center of the handlebars, in addition to the grille-mounted headlights. When you're in the woods at night looking for a downed critter, a lost hunter, or a well-hidden duck blind, this top-mounted light really comes in handy.

Honda FourTrax Foreman Rubicon

I've had the opportunity to drive the Honda FourTrax Foreman Rubicon on extensive tests and must say the machine is one of the best balanced around. It doesn't have too much ground clearance, making it easily maneuverable, yet it's highly stable on sidehills and turns. Still, I felt that the most outstanding feature of this machine is its Hondamatic transmission. The most sophisticated transmission on the market, it provides extremely smooth shifting. A dash-mounted knob switches to one of three electronic shifting programs: D1 for maximum performance; D2 for maximum torque; and ESP, Honda's exclusive Electric Shift Program. The D1 and D2 modes provide continuously variable transmission output. I used D1 for acceleration tests and D2 for the pulling tests, both with good results. ESP, however, allows you to "shift" the Hondamatic with a thumb, using two push buttons. It's designed for hilly terrain littered with boulders and other obstacles. You can switch, on the fly, from performance on the straight runs to torque for slow-speed climbing. Engine braking is also excellent, especially in the ESP mode, switching instantly from performance to the torque needed to brake even on steep hills. The transmission is totally sealed and extremely durable.

Honda FourTrax Foreman Rubicon has the most sophisticated automatic transmission on the market. Three programs are selectable with a switch. (Photo courtesy Honda)

The Honda FourTrax Foreman Rubicon also offers full-time four-wheel drive and a unique torque-sensing, limited-slip front differential that provides superior traction and reduces torque steer for less steering effort. The machine turns like a dream. The unique design reduces engine height, with an underhead camshaft, located adjacent to the cylinder head, an external engine oil tank, and a compact, flat-shaped radiator fan. This ingenious configuration creates an extremely low center of gravity and excellent handling. Turns were quick but with no tilting.

The engine and transmission utilize an unusual multiple scavenging oil system with three pumps to provide a stable oil supply even in diverse riding conditions. Suspension is excellent, with independent double-wishbone front suspension and a steel swingarm, and dual rear shock absorbers. The Hondamatic makes ATV riding a breeze even for first-timers.

Yamaha Grizzly 700 4x4

Absolute control was the feeling I had climbing up the Montana mountainside. Steep and laden with blowdowns and boulders, the climb was indeed a grueling test for the Yamaha Grizzly 700. In four-wheel drive and low gear, the Grizzly steadily climbed up and over all obstacles with ease. This powerhouse never faltered or had any inconsistencies in power or traction. What goes up must come down, and I did—straight down a very steep and well-worn trail next to a purple-painted line fence.

The Grizzly 700 control begins with an industry first, Yamaha Electric Power Steering (EPS). Like me, you probably have doubts as to the feasibility of power steering on an ATV, although the feature has become increasingly popular on boats with large engines. After a full day of demanding ATV test rides, however, I came away for the first time without shoulder, arm, or wrist fatigue. Some of my "older" buddies had the same experience. Although technically complicated, in use the EPS is simple. It's torque sensing; as you turn the handlebars, an electric motor turns on and helps. The harder you turn the handlebars, the more EPS offers assistance. Not only does the Yamaha EPS require less steering effort but, surprisingly, there also seems to be more sensitivity and road feel. An added benefit is reduced kickback. When a wheel hits an obstacle such as a log, rock, or stump, the EPS automatically kicks in. I repeatedly tested this feature on the Montana mountainside. Accidentally catching a

The Yamaha Grizzly 700 introduced an industry first, Yamaha Electric Power Steering (EPS). Plus it has a lower center of gravity with great handling and balance. (Photo courtesy Yamaha)

stump or log end on the outside edge of one wheel, at fairly fast speeds, could easily jerk the handlebars out of your hands. EPS greatly reduces this.

Most ATVs have the gearshift on the right-hand side to ensure that your right thumb is off the throttle when you shift. Yamaha has moved the gate shift lever over to the left, allowing you to shift more easily without removing your right-hand control from the handlebar. I found this especially helpful when cresting a hill and seeing a steep downgrade. Backing off the throttle, braking, and immediately shifting into low range with my left hand was quick and easy. And the three-way on-command 2WD/4WD is easily accessed with your right hand as well. Engine braking is impressive; in several cases, I simply let the ATV, in four-wheel drive and low gear, idle me down the steep hillside, with no additional braking needed.

Differential lock is instantly available with a push button. I found this invaluable climbing over some mine-tailing rock piles. The shift level has been improved, too, using a straight back–forward pattern that makes it easy to shift and see what gear you're in. I did find it somewhat difficult at times to shift into low gear. Several times I had to rock the vehicle a bit to get the gear changed. The redesigned LED display shows gear selection and 2WD or 4WD selection, in addition to speedometer, odometer, dual trip meter, fuel level indicator, and fuel injection lights. The machine is self-diagnostic, with indicator lights to let you know when the systems need to be serviced.

The suspension adds to the control. A fully independent wishbone front and independent rear suspension, both adjustable, provide a great deal of versatility, allowing you to set up the suspension for your particular riding conditions. Up front, travel is 7.1 inches; rear is 9.5. Ground clearance of 11.8 inches provides plenty of up-and-over for obstacles. One interesting suspension change is the redesign of the front and rear A-arms. They feature a new rounded shape that provides more side-to-side ground clearance. Lower mounting points for the A-arms add to a lower center of gravity, making riding balance even more controllable. Redesigning and relocating the fuel tank directly under the seat adds to the lower center of gravity and increased control.

The brakes on the Grizzly 700 are four-wheel hydraulic disc models, one for each wheel. Many ATVs utilize three brakes, one for each front wheel and one to provide braking for both rear wheels. A new master cylinder located front and rear, along with brake calipers for each wheel, gives absolute braking control—as I discovered on some fast test stops.

Of course, the main feature is the Grizzly 700 power plant. Adapted from the Raptor 700R, the Yamaha sport ATV, this power plant moves from the 660cc of the former Grizzly to 686cc. The additional 26cc provides a quicker response and more control with additional power, especially in the lower and midrange power band. Also coming from the Raptor side is the Yamaha Fuel Injection System (YFI). This system, of course, provides for no-choke starting and easier cold-morning starts. YFI, with precise fuel delivery, offers a much quicker throttle response, is cleaner burning, and has greater fuel economy. In my tests, the throttle response was immediate, dumping the throttle brought instant power, and mid- and low-range response was extremely good.

Styling has been changed from the 660 Grizzly to provide a lower center of gravity, centralize mass, and improve handling characteristics. The air box has been relocated from under the seat to the top of the engine. Not only does this provide easier access for maintenance, but the higher intake provides more protection in deep-water crossings as well. There's even a small storage compartment in the front fender. If it were redesigned just an inch deeper, it would hold a standard water bottle. Yamaha has also introduced a SecureMount rack system, making it easy to fit Yamaha accessories to the rack. And the dual 35-watt halogen headlights are bigger.

Yamaha has indeed upped the bar with the Grizzly 700. For all its power, this is one of the most controllable ATVs on the market, even for less experienced riders. And it's an easy but fun drive for the more experienced.

Yamaha Bruin 250

I usually test the latest, greatest in the monster ATVs. This time I decided to go the opposite direction and test a more economical, entry-level model. The Yamaha Bruin 250 provides an economical but high-quality ATV. At only 456 pounds and sitting fairly low, the vehicle provides a very spunky yet easily handled ride, even for beginning adult riders, and is an especially nice fit for smaller-framed adults. The Yamaha Bruin 250 may be a little bear, but it's still mighty tough and has plenty of bite.

This vehicle handles beautifully. Turns are crisp yet smooth. A tight turning radius is one major feature. And the ride is amazingly smooth. The machine has a single swingarm with five-way preload adjustment as rear suspension. This means you can adjust it to your

The Yamaha Bruin 250 is an economical, manual shift ATV that provides a good ride and good performance in a smaller ATV.

weight and/or riding style, or to haul gear if needed. Still, the rear rack capacity rating is 99 pounds—66 pounds on the front rack—so don't count on hauling out a big deer carcass. Seat height is only 30.7 inches, yet the vehicle's frame sits fairly high. The Bruin 250 has the longest-in-its-class wheelbase and a big, thick, comfortable seat. The chassis is full sized, which means it can carry full-sized people and loads with no problem. The racks are well laid out for transporting a variety of items and are wrinkle finished, providing a very good appearance. Toting tree stands, hauling a bag or two of feed, or just scouting or checking on livestock are ideal chores for this machine.

Off-road this is a fun vehicle, nimble as a little bear climbing a tree. Traversing some thick timber, I discovered how easy it is to maneuver around trees, stumps, and logs. Even though it's only two-wheel drive, I easily climbed over small obstacles. And given the vehicle's light weight, even if you do occasionally hang up, it's easy to bounce the machine off and be on your way. Full-sized tires and Grizzly-style bodywork with built-in floorboards provide not only greater ground clearance but also more protection for your feet in rough terrain. The foot pads are rugged and serrated for control.

Braking is crisp and easy, featuring dual hydraulic disc brakes on the front and a fully sealed drum brake on the rear. Rear-wheel braking is accomplished with a foot pedal on the right foot pad and a handle on the left handlebar. Brake the front wheels with a hand-grip on the right. Park is with a simple snap-down button on the left-hand handlebar.

The Bruin 250 has rear-wheel engine braking. Typical of Yamaha, it's extremely good. Transmission is manual five-speed, with automatic clutch and reverse. The first gear is a stump-pulling granny low. In fact, you can run the Bruin in third gear practically all the time, except when you need to do some hill climbing or descending. With the shift lever in forward, the five-speed forward gears are accessed by a foot shaft on the left-hand floorboard side. Reverse can only be accessed from first gear by shifting the lever on the console. Shifting into and out of reverse, however, didn't always work easily—my only complaint about the vehicle.

The engine is a 230cc, four-stroke, single-cylinder, air-cooled SOHC model with a Mikuni 33mm carburetor. There's plenty of spunk beginning in the low torque end and up through the midrange. On the top end, the Bruin scrambles. A DC-CDI ignition system creates dependable starting and provides a consistent spark at all RPMs, resulting in fine engine performance throughout the power band range. An automatic cam chain tensioner reduces engine maintenance and helps to extend engine life. Final drive is shaft, extremely reliable and sturdy, especially for this economical vehicle. The standard trailer hitch is rated for 730 pounds, and I found the Bruin more than adequate hauling a full-sized trailer loaded with steel posts and fencing supplies to the back 40.

The front is built for tough use with a heavy-duty front carry bar and skid plate. A relatively smooth undercarriage adds to off-road durability. A two-step powder-coating process used on the frame also protects against rock and debris damage, adding to the resilience. A rear brake light is highly visible; dual 25-watt headlights provide illumination for low-light and nighttime use. The battery is accessed by simply pulling up a panel under the rear rack. Fenders are large and well designed to protect the rider.

The Yamaha 250 Bruin is an excellent, economical starter ATV. Many families these days have not only two cars but two ATVs as well, and the Bruin 250 makes an excellent second vehicle. In fact, an ideal scenario might consist of the Yamaha Rhino 650 for serious off-road work and play, and the Bruin 250 as a quick jump-on, go-anywhere-to-check-on-things vehicle or for off-road fun.

Suzuki KingQuad 700

Dump the throttle and like a streak of lightning, the Suzuki KingQuad leaps forward. Powered by a 695cc fuel-injected four-stroke, this big-bore ATV provides awesome power. "Today's ATV riders want more power, more comfort, and more convenience from their ATV than ever before," says Glenn Hansen, Suzuki motorcycle and ATV advertising and press relations manager. "Suzuki has responded with the KingQuad 700, which comes with the most-requested high-performance features ever assembled on a big-bore machine."

Testing the KingQuad for about a month on some grueling mountainous trails, I soon saw for myself. It's indeed hot, not only from a standstill start, but especially up in the midrange of 20 to 25 miles per hour, again providing instant response. The top end takes a lot of handling.

The Suzuki KingQuad 700 4x4 is powered by a 695cc fuel-injected four-stroke that provides awesome power. (Photo courtesy Suzuki)

More than 15 years ago, Suzuki made history as the first company to produce four-wheelers with its KingQuad. The original KingQuad began its rule in 1991 as a revolutionary ATV well-known for riding comfort and utility performance. In honor of the popularity and prestige of this early model, Suzuki has built an all-new flagship ATV bearing the KingQuad name.

What gives the new KingQuad its "energy," as well as a more efficient fuel delivery, is the electronic fuel injection system (EFI). Adapted from the championship-winning GSX-R sport bike, EFI offers advantages that include more riding range per gallon of fuel, advanced throttle response, and smoother engine power. You'll notice that there's no choke on the new KingQuad. The electronic fuel injection system provides more reliable and consistent starting in cold- and hot-weather conditions. I gave my KingQuad EFI a good trial as I cranked it up one morning in 10-degree F weather. It started almost instantly. I also test boats for boating magazines, and EFI outboard engines, with their easy-starting features, have quickly become popular. Six sensors in the engine provide instantaneous information to the engine-control module (ECM), which then directs the correct amount of fuel through the injector. No more waste; fuel is used only on demand. Naturally, engine response is quicker with EFI.

More KingQuad features include a continuously variable automatic transmission and a three-mode drivetrain with two-wheel drive, four-wheel drive, and front differential-locked four-wheel drive. The automatic shifting is smooth and powerful, with great downhill braking capability due to the Quadmatic transmission, which uses a centrifugal clutch behind the primary belt clutch. This prevents the belt from ever becoming slack. There's a lot of traction in the KingQuad—as I found in a deep mud hole. I deliberately stopped the vehicle directly in the mud, shifted into 4WD, and dumped the throttle. I popped out of that mud hole like a cork out of a bottle. I found the front differential-locked four-wheel drive extremely helpful in climbing some boulder-strewn hills. I also tested the three-way transmission mode on a log over a trail: The KingQuad nimbly jumped it. Also useful in boulder fields, rocky trails, and log- and stump-littered woodlands is the fully independent suspension system. Each wheel rides smoothly and separately on adjustable shock absorbers. These five-way absorbers make it easy to set the feel of the ride you desire according to terrain and loading of the machine.

Built on a high-tensile steel frame, the vehicle handles extremely well. It's fairly lightweight despite its power, and has a low center of gravity. Turns are crisp—in fact, this is the easiest-turning ATV I've handled. It even turns effortlessly when idling. My wife, Joan, really appreciated this handling ease. The long seat provides lots of room to slide back and forth for balance, with plenty of side feel for those leaning turns. The automatic gearshift is conveniently located and very easy to operate with a simple gate-style design. Braking—done by levers on both handlebars and with a right-foot brake—is extremely good on this machine. Shifting between two- and four-wheel drive is done via a button on the right-hand side of the handlebars. A convenient button located nearby will shift you into front differential lock.

The Suzuki has an aggressive sport-utility styling. High-arched fenders, dual multireflector headlights, and a center-steering-wheel-mounted light add to the appeal; the center light provides illumination wherever the handlebars are turned. Sturdy front and rear racks are powder coated in a nonreflective black finish, which adds not only to the vehicle's good looks but also to its durability. A weatherproof, stowable pocket for cell phones and other small items is positioned on the right-hand side of the console. It is accessed by removing a rubber O-ring-sealed cap. A small toolbox is located beneath the rear rack. The machine is available in three bold colors—Champion Yellow, Flame Red, and Shooting Green.

Arctic Cat Remington Special Edition

Arctic Cat and Remington have combined to offer the "ultimate" hunting ATV with their Big Game Edition. I tested the 650 model on the rugged trails and hills of Missouri's Ozarks at Dogwood Hills Canyon during an Arctic Cat press introduction. This machine is available with a choice of two big-power engines—the 650 V-twin or an all-new 650 H1—and I tried both. The H1 has 641cc, the V-twin 633cc, but both have awesome power. The Big Game Edition I tested had a V-twin.

In addition to the distinctive Remington logo, the Big Game Edition sports a full complement of Arctic Cat's SpeedRack accessories, all designed to attach and detach within seconds to the front and rear racks. Merely slide the accessory in place and set a security pin. Removal is just as easy. The package includes an 11 x 17-inch carryall, bucket holder, fender box, tree stand/bow case holder, gun scabbard kit, brushguard bumper, black handguards, rack basket, portable mounted light, cargo box (in Realtree Hardwoods), and cargo box kit. With the racks and accessories, you can head afield completely equipped for the day, or even longer.

With all the accessories and hunting gear for an extended trip mounted on the Remington Edition, the ATV looks and feels fully loaded. I was interested in seeing how all the extra weight and any change in balance might affect handling and performance. I found that torque was great, with no decrease in performance from low to high end, in climbing hills, or on downgrades. The fully automatic transmission has both high and low ranges and features excellent engine-braking power. The balance on some sidehills was better than expected, but I wouldn't suggest full-power sidehill runs while fully loaded. There was no back-tippiness on hill climbs. The Arctic Cat 650 features a full-lock front differential that transfers engine torque to both front wheels when needed for added traction. This is done with a quick flip of a switch. I only had to use the front differential once during a boulder climb. As I discovered changing from mild trails to rugged runs, switching from two- to four-wheel drive

Arctic Cat Remington Big Game Special Edition is ready to hunt. It comes with the Arctic Cat Speedrack System and a complement of hunting accessories.

is done on the fly via an electric shift lever conveniently located on the right handlebar.

Other features that make the Big Game Edition 650 easy to handle, even fully loaded, are its fully independent suspension, front and back, and its 12.5 inches of ground clearance. The suspension allows all four wheels to articulate throughout the entire range of travel. This definitely helps balance out the loaded ATV. The FIS is a full 10 inches both front and back, and features spring preload shocks. You can set the rear and front in five different positions to customize the suspension to your riding style and terrain as well as the load you're carrying. Arctic Cat also offers an optional sway bar available through dealers as an accessory. Adding one does cause some changes in traction, but it enhances flatter cornering in aggressive trail riding—something you're not likely to do with the fully loaded Big Game Edition.

In my continued tests with Arctic Cat, I've discovered that their vehicles are extremely durable and easy to maintain. This begins with maintenance-free bushings on the suspension and color-coordinated stick stoppers that add protection to the CV boots. A heavy-duty steel frame, sealed engine and magneto, and high-density skid plate all offer protection from the rough-tough, dirty, and muddy life of an ATV.

The 650's new extra-wide fenders offer plenty of protection from mud and water spray. Cat-eye headlights look great and provide great illumination, while integrated full-length plastic floorboards give excellent traction regardless of your riding style. The seat has been widened, and a user-friendly latch lets you access a handy tool tray. Another feature I really like is the sturdy 2-inch automotive-style receiver hitch. The digital instrument pod displays up to 15 different operation information indicators, including mph, odometer, dual trip meters, hour meter, clock, and fuel level.

If your favorite deer or big-game hunting is off-road, in the backcountry, the Arctic Cat 650 Remington Big Game Edition can be a great way of getting there and back.

Bombardier Traxter Semiautomatic

The slogan of the company is "Work then play," and Bombardier makes solid, sturdy ATVs designed for hard work. The Traxter excels in pulling and towing. Part of the reason is that at 755 pounds, the unit is designed primarily for industrial use and provides greater

Bombardier Traxter semiautomatic is a heavy-duty vehicle designed for both work and play. It has the industry's only step-through seating. (Photo courtesy Bombardier)

torque than other ATVs. The unit I tested features a dual shift pattern—semiautomatic and fully automatic. I preferred the semiautomatic because it was easy to change gears while going up and down hills, and around curves, corners, and obstacles, with a simple touch of the finger on the left-hand handlebar.

In automatic, the unit occasionally shifted at unexpected times, but this setting does provide easier riding for those without shifting experience. All Traxter models are equipped with an extremely heavy-duty, constant-mesh, fully engaged gear-drive transmission, which offers maximum efficiency, low heat generation, and reliability.

As an over-fifty rider, I also appreciate the features of this machine designed for hard work by farmers, ranchers, and loggers. You don't have to step over the seat—there's a step-through in front. The Traxter is designed for riders who frequently get off and on, and would be an excellent choice for those with extensive food plots or other landowner chores. The lift-up seat provides fine engine access, while the unit also features a tremendous amount of storage under a lift-up hood in front.

One unusual feature is the self-diagnosing engine. A computer modulates the clutch, which changes from softer to harder for better performance or more pulling power. Add this to the progressive front differential, the independent suspension double A-arm, and the rigid rear swingarm, and Bombardier has delivered a great work vehicle. Take the Traxter on the trail for a fun run, however, and it can offer lots of play as well.

Double-Up ATVs

Most ATVs are designed for use with only one rider; they should never be ridden by more than one at a time. Several manufacturers, however, have developed ATVs specifically for carrying passengers. These feature large wheelbases and special seats.

Bombardier Traxter MAX

It was a blast. First I drove and my wife, Joan, rode behind me. Then she drove and I rode behind her. For years we've been told two can't ride an ATV, and it's true. Riding double on ATVs, even the larger utility vehicles on the market, can be very dangerous—and in some instances it's unlawful. Yes, I know, we've all done it. Go to almost any hunting camp, and you'll probably double up going to your stands, or maybe to scout for turkeys. I'm not sure I've even been on an ATV trail in the past few years without meeting two people riding an ATV. Well, now you can *safely* take your hunting buddy, friend, or spouse with you. The Bombardier Traxter MAX is designed specifically for two riders. After our tests, Joan and I agreed that this is going to be a very popular ATV. I predict that graying ATVers will really appreciate the chance for spouses to ride together, especially on the trail. Parents or grandparents can now safely take along a youngster as well. Bombardier's step-through seat for ease of access is another plus.

The second rider sits forward of the axle, not over it, making the Traxter MAX the most stable ATV on the market. The company challenges you to try it with a big rider, and I invited a big redneck hunting buddy for the test. I really didn't even know he was there. The frame is about 18 inches longer than a standard ATV to give more stability. The tires are one size larger than most machines and have a stance about 1 inch wider. Bombardier has solved several second-rider problems quite handily. If you dump the throttle and the second rider isn't ready or expecting it, for instance, he can be flipped off the back of the unit—but the Traxter MAX has a backrest to prevent this. The second-rider seat is slightly higher than the driver's, too, allowing better visibility for the passenger.

I also test bass boats, and one of their most appreciated features is passenger grab rails and handholds. Bombardier has now built similar ATV hand grabs that extend from the rear rack forward to either side of the second rider. The ATV driver, of course, has the steering wheel to hang on to when running at high speeds; these new passenger assists provide the same for riders, which can be very comforting on turns and rough terrain. The floorboards are designed with two riders in mind, too: The rear portion for the second rider is extended higher, while both driver and passenger have sturdy foot pegs. This allows the second rider to help balance the machine as needed.

The Traxter MAX is classified by the company as a "Super Duty" ATV. It features a gear-to-gear transmission with 10 speeds forward; reverse has low, high, and 2 speeds. Shifting can be manual or automatic. The manual gear-to-gear feature is very important when using the ATV for work, such as spraying. Set the speed at 3 mph, for example, with a certain gear and maintain a steady speed. Then shift into automatic when riding without worrying about shifting. The shifting is, however, very noticeable with a definite *clunk* sound and jump up or down in speed with each gear shift. This is not a slip-style transmission, and it will take some getting used to if that's where your experience lies. ATVers with a manual shift background won't notice as much difference.

The Traxter MAX has an industrial Rotax engine, not a standard ATV engine. It is interesting to note that Rotax has produced more than five million engines for the recreational industry. The two spark plugs should provide a clean ignition, but I had some problems with my unit. I brought it home from the dealer one evening in the middle of a very cold Missouri winter. The next morning, with temperatures at 5 degrees F, I couldn't get the unit to start. A few days later we saw a heat wave of 20 degrees—and I still couldn't get the unit to start. The dealer had provided an extra set of spark plugs; when I changed them, the unit started on the first crank. The dealer explained that the engine will not take any fuel increase while choking without flooding and fouling the plugs, but this tends to correct itself as the engine breaks in. I didn't have any more problems.

The suspension on this ATV is very heavy. This is not an ATV for jumping. However, with Joan driving and me riding, we negotiated an 8-inch log across the trail. With just a bit of coaxing, the vehicle slowly climbed up and over. Joan didn't feel she lost control at any time, and I didn't feel any discomfort. Part of this is due to the Visco Lok four-wheel-drive system, the same as used on the Hummer military vehicle. If one wheel spins, they all spin. The computer-controlled system adjusts power to the wheels at all speeds. This makes it feel like a vehicle with power steering, which is great for creek crossings or climbing banks.

All regular maintenance is under the seat, which removes easily, though it's fairly hefty. The oil, filters, battery, and spark plugs are all easily accessed. The Traxter MAX is equipped with a 400-watt generator system and will run most electrical tools with a converter; or you can easily run any DC accessory. This is a great feature if you're putting up a fence, a tree stand, or even a hunting lodge back in the boonies.

The radiator and fan are located in the rear of the unit, just under the rear rack. Not only does this mean no punctures from sticks or rocks, but it also allows for another neat innovation: The space in the front, under the front rack, is molded into an 8-gallon storage area with a waterproof lid. It is now possible to carry spare clothes, ammunition, or other gear in the dry. I fit a big RedHead day pack in the unit without any trouble. The storage area also has a drain. Filled with ice, it makes a great cooler for a day-trip lunch and drinks. The design is well thought out with the lid recessed under the front rack, so you still have front rack capability as well.

Joan and I were both very impressed with the unit. She has small hands, and the brake lever on the left-hand side was a bit of a reach. This is a hefty, hardworking machine. The Bombardier Traxter MAX was called the "Habitat King" at a recent International Fish and Wildlife Agencies Conference. If you're looking for the ideal habitat/plot ATV that also gets you and your hunting partner, as well as your gear and game, in and out of the woods, this is it.

Polaris Sportsman X2

ATV versatility has become increasingly popular among today's outdoor enthusiasts. With a big cargo bed, the Polaris Sportsman X2 may just be the most versatile ATV on the market. Without taking off or adding any components, it can be used for any number of

Most ATVs are not designed for two passengers. Manufacturers, however, are now producing ATVs with larger wheel bases designed to handle a driver and passenger. Shown is the Polaris X2.

chores, including legally carrying a passenger. The X2 features a "stow and go" second seat that folds into the rear cargo box when you want only one rider aboard. The integrated seating system lets you transform the machine from carrying cargo to carrying a passenger in seconds, with no extra parts to store, tote around, or lose. You'll find raised footrests as well as grab handles on either side of the rear seat for the passenger.

The Sportsman X2 is based on the popular Sportsman 500 platform, providing extreme versatility along with the performance, power, and comfort associated with the Sportsman line. A feature I really liked is the electronic fuel injection (EFI). This not only makes for simple ignition, with no choking needed, but also uses a Throttle Position Sensor (TPS) that ensures a precise throttle response. Although it's a big ATV, the X2 is very quick—as I discovered running some wooded trails with tight turns. Punch the throttle and you'd better be hanging on. The same precise throttle response is just as important in the lower speeds. There is no "stuttering" or slow response at any speed.

The EFI system compensates automatically for changes in altitude and temperature so that the Sportsman X2 will start readily in all conditions, from -25 to 120 degrees F and at altitudes up to 10,000 feet. I also test and write about boats, and the boating industry has widely adopted electronic fuel injection for a number of years. I'm glad to see the ATV industry doing the same. Not only is the response better, but the improved gas mileage is easier on both pocketbook and the environment. Paired with the EFI feature is a liquid-cooled Polaris 499cc high-output four-stroke, single-cylinder engine.

The Polaris Variable Transmission (PVT) is, according to the company, the industry's all-time best-selling automatic transmission. It uses a belt backed by a Polaris lifetime limited warranty. The PVT continually senses engine speed and vehicle torque load and provides the proper amount of power to the drive wheels. The Polaris Engine Braking System (EBS) is also one of the best in the industry. Shut down the throttle on a steep incline and the transmission immediately begins slowing the vehicle. This is not a sudden stop, but a gradual deceleration.

The Sportsman X2 uses Polaris On-Demand All-Wheel Drive. As soon as the rear wheels lose traction, this system automatically engages both front wheels to provide full torque to all four wheels. Power is delivered through a four-wheel independent shaft drive. AWD automatically reverts to 2WD when it's no longer needed. This makes for an extremely responsive system, as I've discovered in my continued tests of Polaris products.

Last year Polaris introduced double offset joint (DOJ) half shafts. These reduce the vibration common with 4WD and improve the ride when you're accelerating, decelerating, running uphill, or otherwise maneuvering in AWD. A switch on the right handlebar allows you to access Versatrac or one of three traction options: Turf Mode, 2WD, or On-Demand All-Wheel Drive for rough terrain. Turf Mode unlocks the rear differential, producing a 20 percent tighter turning radius and turf-friendly operation that is engaged with a dash-mounted electronic switch. The X2 also features front-wheel braking when the vehicle is in AWD mode and the vehicle is operating at speeds below 15 mph. Operating modes are just as versatile as the vehicle itself. Like other Sportsman models, the Sportsman X2 has a wide front-wheel stance and a MacPherson strut front suspension. Front suspension travel of 8.2 inches provides a smooth ride and also better handling, especially under fast and tough riding conditions—the long travel allows the front tires to maintain consistent contact with the ground. The Polaris long-travel Independent

Rear Suspension (IRS)—a fully independent, progressive-rate rear suspension—has 8.75 inches of travel and a high 11 inches of ground clearance. New for the Sportsman X2 is a "rolled IRS" that reduces vehicle squat under acceleration. In my tests, the Sportsman X2 was extremely easy to handle and had a very smooth ride, even under rugged conditions. Climbing over boulders and stumps was easy.

The front rack—with a carrying capacity of 90 pounds—incorporates an integrated composite storage box whose lid has numerous tiedown points and can be lifted for access, even with gear strapped on. One of the major problems with many ATV racks is the round-tube design. You can't really hook tie straps without having them slide around. This rack design solves the problem quite handily. The heavy-duty rear composite cargo box has a 400-pound capacity; it, too, is designed with lots of places to attach tiedowns. If you're toting a cooler or camping gear for that backcountry spot, these are mighty handy.

I like the sturdy, long-handled drum shift, which has a simple in-line pattern that I found very handy when pulling a Plotmaster for planting chores. The shift includes high, low, neutral, reverse,

Polaris X2 4x4 is extremely versatile. The ATV can be changed from a two-seater to a single rider, tool-free, in a couple of minutes.

and park. Sportsman-series lighting has recently been upgraded. In front the high-beam headlights include reflector lens optics that cast a single wide beam. The two bumper-mounted low-beam headlights are reflector lens style to increase brightness. An industry first is the twin work lights, mounted on the rear and controlled by an on–off switch on the headlight pod.

The Polaris Sportsman X2 is indeed one of the most versatile machines on the market. Regardless of your ATV needs, it can be customized to suit. Not only can you transfigure its riding and hauling capabilities, but you can also tailor maneuverability, speeds, and operating modes to suit almost any situation, from easy trail riding to toting stuff across your lawn or hitting the toughest terrain.

Bombardier Outlander MAX H.O. XT 4x4

A couple of years ago Bombardier introduced the first double-rider ATV, their Traxter MAX. The concept is now available on the Bombardier Outlander 400 H.O. (High Output) XT 4x4. This extremely versatile ATV doubles the fun, allowing two passengers to experience the adventure together. Not only is a comfortable seat available for the second rider, but a "sissy" back prevents the rider from flipping backward with sudden forward moves. Sturdy handholds are located on either side of the seat. The rear seat sits slightly higher; convenient raised footboards with a step-up for passengers add to the comfort. The ATV can be converted to a single-seat model with rear storage space by using the optional new modular seat and rack system, which extends the rear space quickly and easily. Tool-free conversion takes a matter of minutes.

A fairly large storage compartment with removable lid is located just behind the second seat. A removable lid in the front provides access to engine coolant fill tubes and has space to attach a small tool repair pack. The front and rear racks are composite materials, handy for securing items with the inevitable rubber shock cords. Well-designed, sturdy tube grilles protect both front and rear lights as well as other parts of the machine.

More features include covered handlebars for protection from brush and wind. The Outlander MAX XT comes standard with chrome rims and a 2,500-pound Warn Winch with handlebar controls.

The MAX series vehicles are a bit longer than most ATVs. The Outlander is 94 inches in length, which translates into a larger turning radius; still, handling is excellent, with turns crisp and easy. The machine nicely balances the second passenger, and driving with two is trouble-free, although less experienced ATV riders should start slow. One of the reasons for the impressive ride and handling characteristics is the innovative TTI (Trailing Torsional Independent) suspension. This provides superior comfort for two over a broad range of terrain and riding conditions.

Bombardier's SST (Surrounding Spar Technology) one-piece perimeter steel frame also benefits two-up riding with its strength, structural integrity, protection, and weight-to-power ratio. The SST frame delivers a narrow-profile bottom runner whose slide-and-glide action allows the 4x4 to ski across obstacles without getting bogged down. I tested this feature by climbing some logs over trails. Braking is quick and sure, with the single lever found on the left-hand handlebar and the foot brake on the right-hand floor.

The Outlander MAX is powered by a Rotax 400cc four-stroke, single, liquid-cooled, four-valve SOHC engine. There is power to spare; engine braking on downhills is excellent. The gearshift is located on the right-hand side of the console and features high, low, neutral, reverse, and park. The only fault I could find with the machine was that the gearshift didn't match the selector notches with

Utility cargo ATVs are a hybrid between the utility ATVs and cargo-hauling utility vehicles. Bombardier Traxter XL has a longer wheelbase than the Traxter ATV, and has a cargo bed box. (Photo courtesy Gerarld Crawford, *Guns & Gear Magazine*)

the selected gears. Still, this problem could probably be easily corrected by a dealer via shift linkage.

With the first two-up ATV and now the versatile Outlander MAX H.O. 400 XT 4x4, Bombardier has also produced the first "dual-personality" ATV. You can use it for double the fun trail riding or serious hauling.

Utility/Cargo ATVs

These units feature handlebar controls, single seating, and the performance of a utility ATV. They also offer a box on the rear for hauling more cargo than standard utility ATVs. Most are also somewhat longer than utility ATVs. Following are a few of the best.

Polaris All-Terrain Pickup (ATP)

Form and function are the basics of design. Form often means beauty, and the Polaris ATP 500 H.O. is indeed a beautiful machine. The model I tested was decked out in an attractive Sportsman green with silver, white, and black trim.

Beauty, however, is also found in performance. The new ATP features the Polaris 500 High Output (H.O.) engine, which has a

The Polaris All-Terrain Pickup (ATP) offers a heavy-duty cargo box with an amazing 400 pound weight limit, yet handles the off-road easily in ATV style.

four-valve, four-stroke engine with counterbalance, 40mm Mikuni carburetor, and electric start with an advanced dry sump lubrication system for long life. In my tests, initial acceleration was extremely good, both from a standstill and in midrange. Top-end speed was also more than adequate for anything most of us casual off-roaders will encounter. Unlike many ATVs, this one starts with the turn of a key only; no button pushing is required. A switch is available for emergency stops. The engine will start in gear with the brake on.

Polaris offers two well-known traditional features with this model. The first is the Polaris Variable Transmission (PVT)—the industry's best-selling ATV automatic. PVT continually senses engine speed and vehicle torque load and delivers the proper amount of power to the drive wheels for each type of riding situation. It uses a spliceless belt backed by a Polaris lifetime belt warranty. The Polaris Engine Braking System (EBS)—also standard—assists in braking on steep inclines and while riding downhill. It makes for excellent engine braking, even on steep and winding hillside trails. Shifting is a straight back-and-forth pattern. The brake must be applied to shift into high as well as park. A parking brake is built into the shift; there's also one mounted on the handlebars.

This machine's second fine feature is the Polaris On-Demand All-Wheel Drive (AWD) system. This system senses when the rear wheels lose traction and automatically engages both front wheels to provide full torque to all four wheels. AWD reverts to 2WD automatically when it's not needed. A thumb switch activates the AWD system and four-wheel independent shaft drive. The Turf Mode in 2WD creates 20 percent tighter turns and less damage to soft terrain such as lawns.

Braking is done with a single lever on the left handlebar, activating all-wheel hydraulic disc brakes. An auxiliary rear foot brake is also available. One handy feature is the Speedo Mode Override switch or reverse limiter switch. This allows you to gain additional power or switch to four-wheel drive while in reverse. The silver-and-white analog/digital instrument cluster is simple to read.

The function comes with the "P" (Pickup). This model offers even more than the traditional Polaris, and has great versatility. Its first extra feature is the heavy-duty, composite dumping cargo box. This box, with an amazing weight limit of 400 pounds, boasts a drop-down tailgate with a strong center latch. It can be dumped with a large lever on either side of the vehicle. The bottom of the box has built-in D-rings for quick attachment of rubber shock cords to tie items in place. The tops of its sides also have convenient built-in handholds that double as tie strap locations. There is even a comfortable seat backrest built into the front edge. The box holds the taillights as well as side reflectors. I had no problems toting out a dandy Missouri buck this past season. As can be expected, the ATP rear suspension is quite beefy, with heavy-duty double coils over shocks. The shocks are fully adjustable to suit the ride and situation. Front suspension is MacPherson strut with a little more than 6.5 inches of travel.

The front rack serves as an enclosed storage space, too. The composite design features a sealed storage box that can double as a cooler, although it's a bit small. Two convenient knobs on the rear of its lid provide easy entry. Convenient built-in D-rings are included; maximum capacity is 90 pounds. The headlights are built into the front rack, and side reflectors add safety. The Polaris traditional third headlight is mounted in the center of the handlebars. This third light is very convenient when you're searching for something—it can act as a spotlight. Turning the handlebars directs the light, irrespective of the direction of vehicle travel. The front of the composite rack acts as the front brushguard. There is no lower bumper or brushguard, leaving the front-mounted radiator extremely exposed. The way I drive a four-wheeler in the Ozarks, I would poke a stick through this radiator the first week. Some sort of stronger guard should be incorporated.

Dual fender storage pockets hold up to 20 pounds of gear each. Accessed by lifting a composite lid on the tops of the fenders, these are great places for items such as gloves, snacks, and binoculars. Polaris has added even more to the versatility with a new easy-to-use rear receiver hitch rather than a simple bolt or ball hole.

It's hard to beat the functionality of the design of the Polaris All-Terrain Pickup. The 500 H.O. model provides plenty of power and performance for anything from roaming the off-roads to toting heavy loads or even pulling big ATV food-plot implements.

Bombardier Traxter XL

This model shares many features with the Traxter MAX model (see page 32). The XL model has a longer wheelbase and comes with a new high-impact plastic box bed with dumping capacity. Its two-stage double-shock rear suspension can carry as much as 600 pounds of payload. The XL also comes with two additional storage containers, one at each wheelbase, for quick access to tools and materials.

Arctic Cat TBX

The TBX is Arctic Cat's version of a pickup truck. The 650 H1 4x4 Automatic TBX features Cat styling body cues and a cargo box with a big payload. The rear dump box offers a 300-pound capacity and has a pickup-style tailgate latch, plus box tilt latches on both sides of the machine. Handy tiedown attachment points are built directly into the cargo box and TBX frame, while integrated rails accept accessory clampdown fixtures. To top it off, SpeedRacks are incorporated into both front and rear, allowing for attachment of dozens of optional accessories. Hauling big payloads is easy thanks to the 650 H1 four-stroke engine, featuring a Duramatic automatic transmission with high–low range. The convenient handlebar-mounted, electronic 2WD/4WD switch is complemented by a full-lock front differential switch. An Auto Electronic Choke enables quick starting.

Several features add to comfort and convenience, including a wider seat (with a simple latch that allows quick access to a new

Arctic Cat TBX features a big cargo box with hand tiedown attachments built right into the box.

Polaris Sportsman drives like an ATV, has a cargo box, and six-wheel drive for go-anywhere capability. (Photo courtesy Polaris)

tool storage tray), a forward-located storage box, a large 5.5-gallon rear-mounted fuel tank, digital instrument pods, and a foot brake system with remote reservoir master cylinder.

Polaris Sportsman 6x6
The Sportsman 6x6 may be the ultimate six-wheeled utility/cargo vehicle for off-road hunting and working. It features a Polaris 500 four-valve, four-stroke, liquid-cooled engine with automatic transmission and on-demand true six-wheel drive with on–off thumb switch. All-wheel hydraulic disc brakes and a right-hand, rear-axle-only auxiliary brake provide stopping power.

The rear suspension has a progressive-rate center swingarm with 6.5 inches of travel; the rear swingarm has scissor stabilizer and 7.5 inches of travel. A durable composite rear dump box is rated for 800-pound capacity.

Arctic Cat TRV Plus
This unique ATV is probably one of the most versatile on the market. It's basically a three-in-one machine: You can ride tandem with a cushy seat for the passenger, remove the seat for single-person mode, or replace the seat with a SpeedRack for tougher chores. Or

Arctic Cat TRV Plus is a great 3-in-1 ATV. In seconds you can switch from double riders to single rider with a rear rack or switch to a cargo box for carrying gear.

you can add a TBX-style box quickly and easily. The model comes with two durable power options—the air- and oil-cooled 400cc four stroke, or the more powerful 650 H1 power plant.

BUYING A NEW ATV

Purchasing an ATV is a personal matter. Some folks like Fords and some like Chevys, and it's the same with ATVs. Some folks are partial to specific brand names. When shopping for a new vehicle, it's always a good idea to buy from a reputable dealer in your area. You should investigate the dealer and talk to other buyers before making your purchase. And make sure servicing is available in case something does go wrong.

Decide what type of vehicle you want or need. Are you looking for an ATV for pleasure riding, or for work around the house, farm, or job site? Do you want a vehicle for accessing remote hunting and fishing spots? Do you intend to break ground for gardens and food plots with your ATV? (If so, you'll need one of the heavier-duty, larger-horsepower models with four-wheel-drive capability.)

An ATV is a major investment. Make sure you purchase from a reputable dealer and ask for a test drive. (Photo courtesy Suzuki)

Don't rush out and buy an ATV just before deer season; it will likely cost more. The best time to buy is usually January. By then you'll be able to get a better deal on a new unit, and in many cases dealers have slightly used units that have been repossessed.

Make sure you test ride the ATV before purchasing. Every model is somewhat different, and it's important to select one that suits your stature, riding style, and needs.

BUYING A USED ATV

Like buying a new ATV, when purchasing a used model it's a good idea to go to a reputable dealer in your area. Ask about the machine's history: Did the same dealer originally sell it new? Is there a service record? How and where was it used? What type of person owned it?

Overall appearance can be a good indicator of the care—or abuse—that an ATV has been given. A machine that is scratched, dented, or has other obvious damage probably has had a rough life. It's a good idea to check the service records as well. Conscientious owners will have their units serviced regularly.

Here are some more things to look for, whether you're purchasing a used unit from a dealer or an individual:

- Check the air filter. If it's dirty, it's likely that the machine hasn't been properly maintained, and engine problems may develop.
- If the machine is a four-wheel-drive model, make sure the 4WD mode works.
- Check to see if the CV boots are torn.
- Check all fluid levels. Low levels and/or dirty fluids can also indicate poor service or abuse.
- Check the tires and wheel bearings, and look for cracks or dents in the wheel hubs.
- Shake the wheels to determine if there is any play in the steering system or bearings.
- Check the brakes, pads, drums, and other parts for wear.
- Make sure all controls and cables work properly.
- Check the shift mechanism to make sure it works.
- Climb on the machine and bounce side to side and back to front to check the suspension for looseness, squeaks, or rattles indicating worn parts.

Of course, you will want to test drive the machine, preferably somewhere other than in a parking lot or driveway.

INSURANCE

ATVs are a costly investment, and accidents can happen. It's a good idea to have insurance on your vehicle to protect your investment and yourself. Various types are available, and—depending on how you use your bike—you may need some or all of them. Talk to your local insurance agent. There are also a number of ATV insurance specialists on the Internet.

Insurance Types

Here are some insurance terms you should be familiar with:

- **Collision** coverage provides protection against damage to your vehicle in the event it collides with another vehicle, the ground, or an object other than an animal. Additionally, most collision policies will also cover the machine if it's damaged while being transported on either a truck or a trailer.
- **Comprehensive** coverage protects against damage to your vehicle not related to a collision, but from events such as hail, theft, fire, wind, flood, and vandalism.
- **Liability** insurance covers you if you ride your ATV off the boundaries of your own property, where your homeowner's policy no longer automatically covers you. Bodily injury liability provides coverage on your behalf to anyone with whom you are involved in an ATV accident that causes injury, sickness, or death.
- **Medical payment** coverage pays medical bills for any operator, regardless of fault, subject to coverage limit and deductible.
- **Property damage liability** covers other people's property if you become legally liable for damage while operating the insured ATV.
- **Uninsured motorist bodily injury** insurance provides coverage for your injuries or death if you are hit by a person who does not have adequate limits to compensate you for your loss. This type of coverage is not available in all states.

- **Uninsured motorist property damage** coverage protects the insured ATV and equipment against damage by an uninsured person who is considered at fault. It's not available in all states.
- **Underinsured motorist property damage** provides coverage for damage to your property if you are hit by a person who does not have adequate limits to compensate for your loss. Again, this coverage is not available in all states.

Some companies offer a discount for taking an approved ATV safety course.

CHAPTER

Understanding Utility Vehicles

U
tility vehicles feature seating for more than one rider, automotive-style driving and handling, and a cargo bed for hauling. They're available in both two- and four-wheel drive as well as selectable drives. These handy models are one of the fastest-growing segments of the off-road vehicle market.

Utility vehicles can be used to haul deer stands and your buddies to the woods, decoys and gear to waterfowl blinds, and seed

Utility vehicles offer either two- or four-wheel-drive capabilities for off-road use. They also provide two-across seating, handle like automobiles, and have beds for carrying cargo and/or persons. (Photo courtesy Yamaha)

and materials to food plots, not to mention pulling tilling implements, spreading fertilizer, and doing other chores. They can be great around the house and farm for numerous hauling chores. I regularly use a utility vehicle for everything from checking on cows to hauling topsoil for the garden and wood for the fireplace. Since utility vehicles are not qualified as ATVs, some of them are also acceptable for limited use on hard surfaces. Some, however, aren't.

HISTORY OF UTILITY VEHICLES

Kawasaki literally created this important and fast-growing segment of the market when they introduced the multiuse lightweight equipment Mule utility vehicle in 1988. The phenomenon began with a few Kawasaki employees who saw a growing need for a vehicle that was simple to operate, could haul cargo, and had the durability of an industrial engine. They made a few sketches and sent them to their engineers in Japan with a simple question: "Can we build this?"

Utility vehicles began with the Kawasaki Mule in 1988; a number of popular models have been produced since.

Kawasaki, well-known internationally for its engineering excellence, responded positively, and the first Mule utility vehicle, the Mule 1000, became a reality. With carlike controls, a trucklike cargo bed, a bench seat, and automatic transmission, the Mule 1000 became an instant success. Farmers, ranchers, industrial workers, and—to Kawasaki's surprise—hunters bought them as fast as Kawasaki's Lincoln, Nebraska, factory could assemble them.

The firm built on this success the following year with the Mule 2010, which had an air-cooled single-cylinder engine with features similar to those found on the Mule 1000, but the important addition of four-wheel drive. New models and features have been added every year. All Mules now feature fully automatic transmission, reverse gear, and dual-mode differential.

These days, several other ATV manufacturers also produce utility vehicles. In addition, a number of golf cart and industrial electrical vehicle manufacturers have also begun to produce gas-powered utility vehicles for outdoor enthusiasts. Let's take a look at some of the top models available.

Kawasaki Mules

The smallest Mule utility vehicles are the Mule 550 and 520, either of which can be loaded into the back of a full-sized pickup. Both share the same chassis and engine, and while the popular 550 is designed for on- or off-road use, the 520 comes with smooth-tread tires for work on smooth surfaces. Either Mule can carry more than 350 pounds and tow 900 pounds.

On a larger scale, the Mule 2500 is a two-wheeled utility vehicle designed primarily for industrial sites. It can carry over 800 pounds in its cargo bed and tow 1,200. The Mule 2520 is similar to the 2500, but is designed for work on smooth surfaces. It treads lightly on smooth, low-pressure tires. Sound-insulating material surrounds the 2520's V-twin engine, making it extra quiet for golf course and resort use.

The Mule 2510 is extremely popular with hunters and other outdoor enthusiasts. It features the same engine, chassis, and hauling capabilities as the 2500, but has the added benefit of on-demand four-wheel drive. The Mule 2510 can be operated in either two- or four-wheel drive and has a high–low speed range; its limited-slip front differential makes it easy to steer when operating in four-wheel drive.

The smaller-size Mules can fit in the back of a pickup, but still offer lots of cargo space. (Photo courtesy Kawasaki)

A diesel model 2510 is also available. It shares the 2510's sturdy chassis and is powered by a 952cc liquid-cooled, three-cylinder diesel engine. Because large segments of the agricultural and industrial communities depend on diesel power for their other equipment, the "Diesel Mule" is a natural fit because it simplifies refueling. Just as important, the diesel engine produces enormous torque yet is extremely durable, a necessity for the kind of work for which the model is used. The Mule 2510 has 6.7 inches of ground clearance and a bed capacity of 1,100 pounds.

The 3000 Series, introduced in 2001, replaced the 2500 Series. There was, however, more than just a name change. The two-wheel-drive Mule 3000, four-wheel-drive Mule 3010, and turf-friendly 3020 feature more dramatic styling that incorporates ergonomically placed controls as well as other changes. The 3000 Series features fashionable pickup truck styling for a strong and modern appearance. At the touch of a button, the hood above the rugged-looking grille can be lifted to reveal a large storage compartment. Fenders are bulged and rounded to provide additional protection from mud and debris. The cargo bed siderails are taller, and new lever latches grace the tailgate for easier operation. Like all Kawasaki utility vehicles, these feature a tiltable cargo bed, four-wheel independent suspension, fully automatic transmission, and bench seat.

Complementing the looks are ergonomically placed, carlike controls. The forward–reverse shift lever is located within easy reach on the automotive-style dash. On the Mule 3010, one convenient lever also permits you to select forward or reverse as well as two-wheel- or four-wheel-drive operation. A sturdy passenger side grab rail is mounted to the cab frame, and a horn and 12-volt DC outlet are standard. In addition, a glove box has been designed into the dashboard, while parking brake and coolant temperature warning lights are easier to see.

The 3000 Series Mule, flagship of the Kawasaki lineup, comes in both turf friendly two-wheel drive and off-road four-wheel drive versions. (Photo courtesy Kawasaki)

Numerous changes were made to the Mule 3000 Series engine and powertrain. Cooling for the 617cc 90-degree four-stroke V-twin engine was improved by the addition of a larger radiator and fan. A digital electronic ignition system optimizes spark timing, and engine efficiency was upgraded by a new double-barrel carburetor with dual intake tracts. A cyclone-type air cleaner is included, as is an air restriction gauge to indicate when the filter needs to be cleaned or replaced. There is an automotive-style fusebox; oil dipstick and oil filler tube are located underneath the seat.

Transferring power from the Mule's engine is a Continuously Variable Transmission (CVT). In conjunction with the engine upgrades, the new CVT provides a wider ratio for more pulling power and quicker acceleration. The dependable, low-maintenance shaft drive transfers power to a dual-mode differential that can be locked to maximize rear-wheel traction, or unlocked to minimize ground disturbance when making tight turns.

The chassis of the Mule 3000 Series has stiffer springs for increased ground clearance, and the de Dion rear-leaf spring suspension is designed to carry heavy loads, yet provides a smooth ride when the cargo bed is empty. Self-adjusting hydraulic drum brakes at all four wheels ensure progressive stopping power and have extra flanges with upgraded seals to keep out mud and water. New rear-wheel bearings are also more durable and have new seals for better protection from water.

Other features include mounting tabs on the frame for easy installation of a winch, 23-inch tires for the 3000 and 3010 models, and stiffer springs on the independent strut-type front suspension. Bodywork color is molded in to help prevent scuffing.

The Mule 3000 Series can carry 803 pounds in its steel cargo bed and tow 1,200 pounds. The Mule 3000 and 3010 have 7.2 inches of ground clearance.

Kawasaki 3010 Trans4x4

One of the most popular toy fads is Transformers—those ingenious creations that change from a car to a creature simply by turning and twisting different portions. The Kawasaki 3010 Trans4x4 brings the Transformer concept to the big "toys." The Trans4x4 is the world's first four-passenger 4x4 off-road utility vehicle that can be changed in a matter of minutes into a two-passenger vehicle with an extended cargo bed.

Kawasaki 3010 Trans 4x4 is an extremely versatile utility vehicle. The vehicle converts from a two-seater with cargo to a four-seater with cargo in a matter of minutes.

I've tested almost every Mule utility vehicle on the market, and I enjoyed trying out this model as well. When I got my trial vehicle, I was just beginning a fence-building operation and found the machine extremely handy for toting tools and supplies. Based on the popular Mule 3000 series, the new Mule Trans4x4's spacious four-passenger cab easily accommodates four adults. If you want to haul your hunting buddies to the blind, tote upland game hunters, or just trail ride with the family, the four-passenger mode is great. The dual bench seats are extremely comfortable; both front and rear seats feature two retractable seat belts. In addition, padded passenger grab handles are found both front and rear. There is plenty of footroom for the backseat, with a spacious floorboard. But with a couple of quick adjustments, you can fold down the rear bench seat and extend the cargo bed forward to increase the bed size to 48 x 50 inches and the cargo capacity to 800 pounds. When you want to transform the vehicle back into four-passenger mode, the same quick adjustments are made in reverse. In the four-passenger mode, the cargo capacity is 400 pounds with a bed size of 38 x 48 inches—still plenty of room for gear. What makes this all work is that the traditional Mule overhead tubing construction is simply extended back to provide dual seating protection. The cargo bed front shield is moved back and forth to transform the vehicle, a brilliant idea of Kawasaki engineers.

The wheelbase of the Mule 3010 Trans4x4 is 11.6 inches longer than that of the Mule 3010 4x4, and this translates into a wider turning radius. I tested the 3010 on some winding trails, however, without any problems. Handling was extremely good thanks to the rack-and-pinion steering system. The ride is a very smooth, traditional Mule ride. This is due to the MacPherson strut front suspension, combined with a heavy-duty de Dion rear suspension. Twenty-three-inch tires add to the smooth performance.

The Mule 3010 Trans4x4 utilizes the same power train as the Mule 3010 4x4. Its liquid-cooled industrial V-twin engine has a proven record for hardworking reliability. In my tests, I really appreciated the quietness. The Mule is definitely the least noisy utility vehicle on the market. The engine produces exceptional torque at low engine speeds. I had to pull logs and debris out of the way during fence clearing, and appreciated this machine's low-speed power. With the optional Kawasaki tow hitch, the Trans can tow up to 1,200 pounds.

One thing I didn't like about the Mule, however, was that same tow hitch. It requires special Kawasaki equipment, rather than the standard receiver hitch frame that most other utility vehicle manufac-turers have now gone to. With this you can simply pull the hitch out of your vehicle receiver and switch over to an ATV or utility vehicle. The engine powers the Kawasaki continuously variable transmission (CVT) for easy handling in almost any condition—as I discovered in tests that ranged from climbing steep mountainsides to crossing ditches and climbing over a rocky mountaintop bench. The CVT has been fine-tuned for the Trans's higher passenger and cargo capacity, and features high and low ranges, plus reverse. You can select either two- or four-wheel-drive operation, with power being transferred to a shaft-driven dual-mode differential and limited-slip front differen-tial. One of my major tests for this longer-wheelbase vehicle was a fairly steep creek crossing that had to be approached at a 45-degree angle. This means one of the front wheels is off the ground during the crossing. With the limited-slip front differential, I had no prob-lems, even though the crossing was a bit tippy. On the other hand, with the extended chassis, Kawasaki engineers were able to increase fuel capacity nearly 20 percent, from 5.3 gallons to 6.4 gallons. And this brings up one other small quirk I don't like. To know what the fuel tanks holds, you have to fold forward the front seat for a visual check of a manual gauge. With a utility vehicle of this quality and caliber, I would like to see an on-dash fuel gauge. One feature, the hour meter, now starts when the engine is started. And, as I discov-ered on a somewhat deeper creek crossing, the high breather of the Mule, located up in the overhead tubing, is important.

The same carlike controls found on the other 3000 Series Mule utility vehicles make it extremely easy to drive. Braking power is provided by four hydraulically operated, self-adjusting drum brakes that are sealed to protect from water, mud, and other de-bris. The model I tested was traditional Mule green; a camo ver-sion is available.

I can see an almost unlimited range of possibilities for the Kawasaki Mule 3010 Trans4x4. In addition to the ability to transport several hunting partners to their stands or blinds, a family of four could also head off-road, yet tote a tent and other camping gear for a weekend of fun. Farmers and ranchers will welcome the extra cargo-carrying capacity of the vehicle, yet be able to take along family or friends for fun "chores" or recreational activities. I'm sure industrial buyers appreciate the versatility. You may just want to try the "big-toy Transformer" now on the market.

Bobcat 2200 4x4 Utility Vehicle

Bobcat is well-known for producing high-quality industrial equipment, and their 2200 utility 4x4 is not only tough but also one of the easiest-driving utility vehicles out there. It's the only vehicle in its class equipped with automatic locking differentials that engage immediately when a wheel loses traction. There are no buttons to push, no gears to shift. The system, called IntelliTrak, provides power to all four wheels as needed, preventing one, two, or three wheels from spinning without the fourth. "All four wheels must spin together in low-traction conditions," says Brad Claus, Bobcat utility product manager. "These traction characteristics give the 2200 exceptional climbing ability and off-road performance."

As noted, the IntelliTrak drive system engages and disengages the 4x4 and differential lock automatically, so it requires no extra levers, creating a very simple operation. This also eliminates the need to stop the vehicle, allowing the 2200 to stay in motion when mud or snow is encountered. In my tests, I found driving and handling of the Bobcat extremely easy, as was turning with the IntelliTrak system—the automatic locking differentials engage when needed, but disengage when turning. As a result, the 2200 not only gives great off-road traction, but also turns lightly on turf and pavement without causing damage to turf, tires, or drive components. The only fault I could find with the drive system is that the CVT belt is partially exposed. A shroud covers most of it, but some water situations may cause problems. I did, however, make several creek crossings without any problem.

The rack-and-pinion steering was simple to use. To add to the ease of driving, the steering wheel is fully adjustable, and the driver's seat moves forward and back. Both my nephew's 6-foot-6 and my own 5-foot-8 frames were easily accommodated in our tests. The bucket seats simply lift off to provide access to the battery and other components. These high-backed seats are extremely comfortable, sit up high, and have two cup holders between them. A four-point roll-over protective structure (ROPS) and retractable seat belts add to the safety. The more I test utility vehicles, the more I appreciate the ROPS, which not only protects my health but also beats the brush and low-hanging limbs away in timber or brush. A cab enclosure is available as a dealer-installed accessory.

This new utility vehicle from the Bobcat Company is made with a durable corrosion-resistant aluminum chassis. The all-aluminum tubular frame provides a long-lasting frame and makes the 2200 lightweight as well as strong. The gas model weighs 1,361 pounds; the diesel, 1,433 pounds.

I tested the diesel model, which has a 20-horsepower, 719cc Kubota D722 engine. Although extremely powerful, it is fairly loud. There is no hesitation, with a smooth transition of power throughout the power band. Shifting is with a single lever on the dash. The parking brake is automotive style: You push on the pedal to apply, pull on a dash-mounted handle to release. I discovered that the Bobcat 2200 has extremely good climbing ability, but it doesn't have engine braking. The four-wheel hydraulic brakes, however, provided more-than-adequate stopping power.

The bed on the test model was all aluminum for long use and light weight. It was a manual-lift model, and the first thing I would add is the optional power lift. Filled with dirt, rocks, or other heavy materials, it isn't easy to hoist. Mossy Oak camo covered the hood of my test model; camo seat covers and side panels are also available. A 2-inch receiver hitch is standard.

Kubota RTV900R Diesel Utility Vehicle

When one of the most successful tractor manufacturers steps into the utility vehicle market, you can bet on a good product, and the new Kubota RTV900R is indeed quality built. Quality begins with a very powerful 21.6-horsepower, three-cylinder, water-cooled D902 diesel engine. Kubota diesel engines meet EPA standards and are extremely efficient. According to the company, they burn up to a third less fuel than equivalent gas engines. The engine is capable of driving the vehicle up to 21 mph. With the preheat starter, I found the vehicle easy to crank up even in below-freezing weather. Diesel engines are typically louder than most gas engines, and this one was indeed on the noisy side, with a sound level (dBa) rating of 87 at the operator's ear.

The RTV900R utilizes Kubota tractor transmission technology and components to create a unique utility vehicle Variable Hydro Transmission (VHT). The VHT provided great performance in climbing hills, pulling power, and especially braking on hills during tests. In fact, the transmission is so quick, it takes a bit of getting used to. If you let off on the accelerator pedal too quickly, the immediate transmission "stopping" response will just about throw you into the dash. When slowing down, it's important to let off on the accelerator pedal gradually, a technique that is learned very quickly.

Kubota RTV900R Diesel utility vehicle has a unique Variable Hydro, tractor-style transmission and a 21.6 hp, three-cylinder, water-cooled diesel engine.

Unlike most UTVs, the Kubota has a three-range transmission of low, medium, and high, plus reverse. I did find the shifting lever a bit stiff to operate, but the dealer had explained it would be stiff until broken in. Shifting from two- to four-wheel drive is accomplished with a sturdy lever found near the gearshift on the console. The RTV has a rather unusual dual-operating differential lock. If one of the rear wheels should slip, simply step on the differential lock pedal located in the floorboard, near the driver's seat. Both wheels will then turn together, reducing slippage. Differential lock is maintained while the pedal is depressed. You can also pull the differential lock hold button, located near the side of the driver's seat, while depressing the pedal. The lock is then maintained even if your foot leaves the pedal; it's released when the pedal is depressed again.

Pulling power in low is awesome, and in high range the vehicle runs at a fairly good clip. Handling is excellent, and response quick, thanks to the hydraulic power steering. The RTV900R is the first in its class to be equipped with fatigue-reducing full-hydraulic power steering. You can literally drive it with a couple of fingers.

Another feature I appreciate is the hydraulic dumping cargo bed. The hydraulic lift system is heavy duty and extremely fast. It enables easy dumping of even a full heavy load simply by operating a single lever next to the seat. This feature is standard on Work Site, Turf, and all Recreational models starting with serial number 31112 and above. The bed can also be operated manually if desired. The bed is large (52 inches wide, 46.7 inches long, and 11.4 inches deep), and features a diamond-plate steel construction that will handle the toughest materials. This unit is well built and easily handles a load. The cargo bed has a load rating of 1,102 pounds or 16 cubic feet. The tailgate latches operate with the pull of a finger. I especially liked the tailgate suspending cables that hold the gate out level or can be unhooked to drop it completely.

The wet disc brakes operated extremely well, even on some fairly steep downhills—very light in response. The parking brake is a lift lever on the left-hand side of the driver's seat, and a parking brake light is located in the "Easy Checker" on the dash. The latter is another useful addition—an instrument panel with all the features of an automobile dash, including parking brake, electrical charge, engine oil pressure, prestart, hydraulic outlet (if equipped), and hazard or turn signals if equipped. A speedometer is also found in the dash. The console has two generous-sized cup holders, one on each side, but there is no glove box.

The bench seat is contoured and generously padded. It will easily accommodate two large adults. The bottom folds forward, revealing a small tool "shelf" beneath. A separate seat backrest is provided. Dual safety belts and side grab rails offer extra protection. An OSHA-approved roll-over protection system (ROPS) and two seat belts are standard features. A sturdy mesh screen adds to the safety, and also offers some protection from overhead limbs. In addition, the dealer installed a canopy top over the unit I tested for further weather and limb protection.

One aspect many don't appreciate unless they run woodland trails in summer is that the front uprights break up the myriad spiderwebs found in these corridors. One young lady friend of mine refused to go any farther on an ATV when she came back with spiderwebs in her hair and face. The uprights also provide a grab handle, making it easier for oldsters to get up into the vehicle. A sturdy grab handle is located on the passenger's side.

The bulldozer-tough, heavy-duty reinforced steel front bumper is built to take a lot of abuse. Ground clearance is 8.3 inches at the lowest point, the rear axle, and I found it more than adequate for serious off-roading. The ride was pleasant, with no stiffness or bounciness. This is due to the relatively long wheelbase, wide-treaded tires, and independent, MacPherson-strut-type suspension on the front. The rear features a semi-independent de Dion axle with leaf springs and shock absorber.

The rear tow bar is highly sturdy, but the receiver hitch is the smaller 1.5-inch size, rather than the standard 2-inch automobile size many ATVs and UTVs are now adopting. A front trailer hitch pin is also included, which allows for greater maneuverability in confined areas. The RTV900R model I tested had one other quite unusual feature: tractor-style hydraulic hose hookups for use with hydraulic tools, including log splitters and some discs. The RTV900 is available in standard bright Kubota orange in General Purpose, Work Site, or Turf models, or in the Recreational camo version I tested.

Polaris/Browning Ranger XP

Brand partnering has become increasingly popular, and the latest pairing of Polaris, Mossy Oak, and Browning will definitely be of interest to hunting enthusiasts. Browning has made much in the past of their logo, and having it displayed on an ATV or utility vehicle can provide the owner with a very distinctive vehicle. I chose the Polaris/Browning Ranger XP 4x4 utility vehicle for a test. This limited-edition machine has several additional features that make it not only more versatile than the standard Ranger, but more striking as well. First is the appearance, featuring a Mossy Oak New Break-Up design on the hood, dash, and side panels of the dump bed. I liked the use of Mossy Oak camouflage on the wheel rims as well. Distinctive Mossy Oak and Browning decals add to the appeal. The bench seat back features the Browning logo stitched into the black/brown/marsh green upholstery, a very elegant design. There's no-shine, wrinkle black paint on the bumpers, screens, and cab frame. The cab frame is the traditional, sturdy Polaris Ranger design featuring headrests, seat side guards, and a passenger hand-hold. The limited edition features Carlisle PXT Off-Road tires to

Polaris/Browning Ranger XP has Mossy Oak Break Up panels and the distinctive Browning Logo. Features a Warn winch, dual gun scabbard, and comes with a Polaris 700 twin-cylinder EFI engine.

provide superior traction for deep-mud situations. Another great feature is the 4.0 Warn Winch, which has 4,000 pounds of pulling power and 55 feet of 7/16-inch cable. A dual gun scabbard with Lock & Ride mount comes with the Browning Edition.

The XP Browning Edition features the standard Polaris 700 twin-cylinder engine with 683cc. The Electronic Fuel Injection (EFI) engine is easy to start under all types of conditions, with no choking required, and is cleaner running with less fuel consumption than carbureted engines. Turn the key and the distinctive Ranger "rumble" is immediate. In my off-road tests, the engine performed great throughout the power range. Top speed was 43.4 on my radar gun, fairly fast for a big, sturdy utility vehicle. Response is immediate thanks to the Throttle Position Sensor (TPS) in the EFI system.

The automatic Polaris Variable Transmission (PVT) quickly responds to both engine RPM and vehicle torque requirements, providing extremely smooth shifting and great engine-braking power on downhill runs. The Ranger 4x4 also has the Polaris On-Demand All-Wheel Drive. I tested this feature on a forested trail strewn with logs and branches. When the system is in AWD mode and senses rear-wheel traction loss, it automatically transfers torque to both front wheels, engaging them in addition to the rear wheels for true four-wheel drive. I tested the system on a twisting trail that had some loose gravel and again found the control outstanding. The Polaris electronically activated lockable rear differential is operated by the push of a button on the dash, engaging for rough terrain or disengaging for those times when you want smoother handling and less turf damage.

Suspension on the Ranger 4x4 consists of an improved MacPherson strut, a long-travel independent front suspension, and an independent rear suspension that has 9 inches of travel. I found the vehicle to ride extremely well, both when it was carrying little weight as well as loaded full of wet dirt.

The dash and operating controls are well laid out, featuring a straightforward rearward shift lever. A small, open storage compartment is located on the driver's side; a glove box with a foam water seal on the passenger's side. Molded cup holders are available for both driver and passenger. There is also lots of enclosed storage space. The front has a lift-up hood that provides access to toolbox storage, while the space beneath the driver's seat opens to the side for another roomy compartment.

The big composite dump box on the Ranger holds 13 cubic feet and has a cargo payload of 1,000 pounds. The box is big enough to hold a standard pallet and also has drainholes for wet materials. Self-cleaning hinges were much appreciated. One of the problems with many dump beds is debris, such as sand, gravel, wood bark, and chips, lodging in the hinge area. This system alleviates the problem. The pickup-style latch, located in the center of the tailgate, is also easy to operate, even one-handed. The Polaris Lock & Ride Cargo System featured on the cargo bed provides versatile cargo hauling. A full range of Polaris accessories is available to attach to the cargo box in less than 10 seconds.

Arctic Cat Prowler XT

A new cat is on the prowl with Arctic Cat's Prowler XT, a full-featured utility vehicle that's versatile but also designed with plenty of power and off-road maneuverability. I tested the Prowler at Dogwood Canyon Nature Park straddling the Missouri–Arkansas border. This park has a beautiful trout stream with lots of waterfalls, but—more

Arctic Cat Prowler is a unique side-by-side UTV with ATV handling, bucket seats, and a 641cc, four-stroke engine.

important for ATV testing—a full 7-mile Ozark trail system provides lots of hills to climb and descend, as well as switchbacks and creeks to cross. The Prowler XT came through like its namesake.

The folks at Arctic Cat stressed that they all drive ATVs, using them hard in their Minnesota winters for hunting, ice fishing, and even plowing their driveways. Many of the exclusive UTV features found on the Prowler XT are the result of down-home use by the same people who design and build the machines.

The Prowler utilizes a 641cc, four-stroke, single-cylinder machine that provides more than enough torque whether you're climbing steep hills, going downhill, or towing. The liquid-cooled engine is produced by Arctic Cat in their state-of-the-art manufacturing facility, and features a 36mm Keihin carburetor with an automatic choke. I appreciated the latter feature, which would definitely add to the convenience in cold climates. The liquid-cooling system has a high-capacity radiator and thermostatically controlled cooling fan that provides consistent engine operating temperatures. The engine drives a Duramatic automatic transmission with a long-life, maintenance-free belt, and the

CVT transmission provides low, high, neutral, and reverse. Automatic shifting was extremely smooth; the engine showed great torque throughout the power band. On the top end, the Prowler moves like a fast cat. Cast-aluminum 14-inch wheels with color-matched inserts are standard just as on the Arctic Cat LE model ATVs. Goodyear MTR 26 x 9.25 front tires with 26 x 11.25 MTRs on the rear provide excellent traction under all kinds of conditions. This was evident on some muddy creekbottom runs. High floorboards kept my feet dry in water crossings.

The controls and cockpit are well laid out so everything is reachable. Two- or four-wheel drive is electrically selectable with a full-locking front differential that is manually operated. A reverse override button is located on the center console for quicker reverse speeds. Rack-and-pinion steering makes for easy turning in both two- and four-wheel-drive modes. The digital gauge display has 14 operation indicators, including mph, odometer, dual trip, hours, clock, fuel level, and gear position. A red display offers better night-time readability.

Foot-operated front and rear disc brakes provide great stopping power. A foot-operated mechanical parking brake is well positioned. One of the great features is the fully independent suspension. Both front and rear suspensions are fully independent; both have a double A-arm design. This allows you to take the Prowler over even the knurliest of obstacles—as I discovered climbing some rock-strewn trails. The suspension has adjustable spring preload shocks and 10 inches of front and rear travel. Spring preload adjustable shocks are used on all four corners for the ultimate in terrain and load adjustability. This allows for a 12.5-inch ground clearance, providing for great off-roading. A rear-mounted sway bar improves trail driving for the UTV design.

The cab of the Prowler XT is equipped with dual bucket seats and driver/passenger seat belts, a center console with two drink holders, and dual 12-volt accessory plugs. The open-air cab provides limb and brush protection along with various storage compartments, including a dash-mounted tray shelf and an easily accessible molded tool kit located under the passenger's-side seat. I like the glove box with door that opens up instead of down, as is found on many UTVs. A big storage compartment under the hood can hold 25 pounds of hunting supplies or tools and can even double as a cooler to store ice or drinks.

The composite cargo bed will tote up to 600 pounds and has a user-friendly, truck-style gate latch. The cargo box resists rusting and denting and also acts as a dump box with the pull of a lever located behind the driver and passenger seats. It's very easily operated. Another great feature is the 2-inch, automotive-style receiver hitch found both rear and front. This allows you to remove the 2-inch automotive receiver and switch to the Prowler.

Yamaha Rhino 660 SxS

Utility vehicles have become increasingly popular with ATV users and especially hunters. With side-by-side seating and a cargo bed, they provide transportation for two people to get to a hunting spot or camping area, packing in needed gear and then packing out the game. Yamaha jumped into the utility vehicle market in a big way with their Rhino 660, the flagship model of their new Side-by-Side (SxS) lineup. Nimbler and with more off-road aggressiveness than the typical utility vehicle, the Rhino performs more like an ATV, but still provides utility vehicle capabilities. It has all the features found on the Yamaha top ATV models—exclusive Ultramatic automatic transmission, a patented On-Command 2WD/4WD system with differential lock, and independent front and rear suspension.

Power for the Rhino comes from the same proven power plant of the Yamaha Grizzly 660. The five-valve 660cc liquid-cooled engine, with 42mm carburetor, has more than enough muscle. In my tests, I found the throttle response extremely quick. Living up to its name, the Rhino is one fast and aggressive beast. Hit the accelerator pedal from a dead stop and there's an instant feel of power as the machine leaps forward. Midrange and top end are also fast. There's plenty of torque on the bottom end, so the hauling and towing capabilities are great.

The On-Command 2WD/4WD drive system has differential lock; a button located on the dash allows you to get power to all four wheels with a single push. The Yamaha Ultramatic automatic transmission operated extremely smoothly in my tests. This proven transmission provides constant tension on the drive belt, which cuts down on wear and tear. More important, however, the constant tension prevents the free-wheeling sometimes found on other machines when going downhill. The Rhino all-wheel engine braking is superb when going downhill or hauling heavy loads. This has been a favorite feature of mine on all the Yamaha top ATV models as

More nimble and with better handling than most UTVs, the Yamaha Rhino 660 SxS has all the features found on Yamaha top ATVs, plus bucket seats for two and lots of cargo space. (Photo courtesy Yamaha)

well. Additional braking power is supplied with four-piston hydraulic brakes on both the front and rear of the machine.

One feature that makes the Rhino a standout in the utility market is the fully independent front and rear suspension. There's more than 7 inches of suspension travel on all four corners of the vehicle, combined with 12.1 inches of ground clearance. This means it can tackle terrain that's tough even for standard ATVs. I crawled over logs, boulders, and stumps with ease. The suspension also translates into a very smooth ride. Handling is extremely good, again thanks to the suspension. The Rhino sits up fairly high, and visibility is fine. Fast turns up and down rocky trails proved the machine's mettle in my tests. And all four suspension corners have five-way preload adjustment capability. This means you can adjust the load to suit, including heavy cargo loads in the rear if needed.

Seating consists of very comfortable bucket seats with seat belts. Headrests are built into the steel roof support system for additional safety. The seats are removed by lifting a lever in front. A fairly large open area beneath the driver's seat could be used to hold a toolbox or other emergency gear. The dash and controls are easily accessed; the instrument panel provides 4WD indicator lighting and gear selection along with park. Fuel level is determined by a sight slot in the front of the tank and beneath the passenger's seat. Lighting consists of dual 30-watt Krypton Multireflector headlights and dual 21.5-watt brake lights.

The Rhino offers several creature comfort features, including a glove box cover with a latch, tailgate supports that hold it flat in the open position, a smooth "skin" on the inside of the tailgate for easier loading/unloading of cargo, and tiedown hooks in the bed. The model I tested had a rubber floor mat in the cargo area as well. Larger CV joints in both the front and rear have been incorporated for added durability in extreme conditions. A new air-intake system has been designed to assist in bringing in fresher, cooler air to help reduce the frequency of filter changes, as well as providing increased splash protection. The cargo bed, although smaller than some utility vehicle beds, will haul up to 400 pounds of additional gear. One feature I really liked was the gas-assisted tilt. Release the lever and the bed almost tilts by itself when unloaded. The tailgate latches are sturdy and easily worked. The standard "2" receiver hitch means you can take the same hitch right off your truck or SUV and use it for all your towing needs with the Rhino, whether it involves pulling a trailer or hauling a tree stand.

The Rhino is very distinctive and eye catching, especially in the Realtree High-Definition Hardwoods camouflage on the model I tested. The molded hood and flared fenders add to the good looks. Hand grab bars on the upper steel frame are welcomed by us older grayhairs. The seats also have a hand grab/restraint bar on each side. A waterproof, automotive-style DC outlet enables you to use portable electronic devices such as GPS and searchlights.

The gearshift, located on the center console, is easily worked and features a high and low range, along with neutral and reverse.

A simple lever snaps over the 2WD/4WD button on the dash to engage the front differential lock. The parking brake, located next to the gearshift, however, is kind of wimpy, and not necessarily easy to use. In fact, the end cap came off a couple of times in use.

With its high, off-road looks, aggressively molded body, and sturdy steel roof support, the Yamaha Rhino 660 looks as tough as its namesake and is ready for work, play, or serious off-road chores. With great performance and the ability to haul two people plus gear, in my opinion this machine provides an impressive mix of automotive-style operation and ATV-like performance.

John Deere Trail Gator HPX 4x4

It's common knowledge that gators are mean, and the John Deere Trail Gator just got a whole lot meaner. I've tested the various Gator models over the years and found them, although great utility work vehicles, not much fun. They just couldn't compare performance-wise with most other 4x4s on the market. The newer line of John Deere High Performance Series Gators are indeed fun, however, as well as maintaining the usual John Deere level of durability and versatility. The HP models—the Gator HPX, HPX 4x4, HPX Diesel, HPX 4x4 Diesel, and Trail Gator HPX 4x4—all are designed to flank the existing Gator lineup and create a new standard of work-related performance. I tested a Trail Gator HPX 4x4 on my Ozarks hill farm. This spread has plenty of challenges and conditions ranging from mud holes to creeks, steep hills, and lots of wooded trails, some twisting and turning up and down.

The Trail Gator 4x4 turned in a very good performance in all counts. The Gator HPX, HPX 4x4, and Trail Gator HPX 4x4 models are all equipped with 20-horsepower, 617cc, four-cycle Kawasaki gasoline engines. All models have a top ground speed of 25 mph, with a two-range transmission that also allows for superior low-speed pulling capabilities. This is one quick gator. The Trail Gator comes with high-performance, all-terrain tires, a brushguard, and a fully enclosed clutch. This allows it to traverse mud and water areas without the belt slipping. The front brushguard is extremely heavy duty and adds to the aggressive appearance of the vehicle. A hand-operated rear differential lock provides even more go-anywhere capability. The Gator is stopped just as quickly with all-wheel hydraulic disc brakes.

The John Deere Trail Gator HPX 4x4 is a greatly improved, more off-road style UTV than previous models, with lots of spunk, great handling, and, of course, John Deere cargo capability and strength.

Although the HP Gator is exciting, it lives up to its John Deere workhorse legacy. It has a rugged front and rear suspension, and the industry's only high-tech hydroformed steel frame. The latter is the same style used in heavier-duty pickup trucks. With a 1,300-pound payload capacity, it can haul lots of wood, soil, gravel, feed, hay, tree stands—pretty much anything for the farm, ranch, hunting lodge, or outdoor enthusiast.

I was impressed by several design features. The first is the easy-access fuel fill tube located to the side of the driver's seat. A readily seen mechanical fuel gauge is located next to the fill tube. The choke knob is also located in the same area and is easily reached when starting the engine cold. Also helpful is the breather filter located just under the passenger's seat and simple to access for maintenance. The seats are bucket style, very comfortable; the driver's seat is adjustable. Both tilt forward to prevent rainwater from collecting, and the area under the passenger's seat holds the battery and fuse box. Cup holders and a small gear shelf are located on the floor between the seats. A 12-volt plug is found on the dash. The passenger's side has a large, deep open glove box as well as a handhold, something well appreciated by passengers in rougher terrain. Shifting is accomplished via a gearshift located between the two seats. The rear differential lock as well as the hand-parking brake are found in the same area. The four-wheel/two-wheel shift is with a handy paddle-style lever in the center of the dash.

Steering is rack and pinion; I felt no play or looseness. Handling is precise and quick. The front suspension features a MacPherson strut with single A-arm and 4.24 inches of travel. The rear suspension is coil over shocks (two) with 3 inches of travel. A heavy-duty guard around the rear differential and axles provides great protection for those unavoidable rocks and stumps. Stick-stoppers are located on the front arms.

The dump bed is made of heavy-duty steel and has a user-friendly hinged tailgate. Manual dump comes standard, but the unit I tested came with the optional power lift. Regardless of the utility vehicle, a power dump bed can be extremely handy. It can be a bit hard on your back to manually lift and dump a bed filled with heavy materials.

The mean and tough John Deere Trail Gator HPX 4x4 is work and play ready, a great utility vehicle for just about any chore you can imagine. A wide range of Deere accessories is also available for the new Trail Gator.

E-Z-GO 4x4

It was all Joan's fault. We were testing an E-Z-GO utility vehicle several years back for *American Rifleman*, and my wife drove the vehicle into a creek. Actually, she drove it into the creek for me to photograph. Unfortunately, when the exposed drive belt went underwater, the vehicle stopped. Water shot a couple of feet between the bed and cab as Joan floored the accelerator, but that vehicle wasn't going anywhere. That was the only criticism we had of the E-Z-GO at the time.

E-Z-GO Textron has now produced the company's first four-wheel-drive utility vehicle, the ST 4x4 Off-Road Utility Vehicle. This newer 4x4 has a heavy-duty, single-ratio Continuously Variable Transmission (CVT) with drive clutches protected by an environmental cover. You don't have to worry about the belt slipping in wet conditions with this design. The front differential is surrounded by rugged frame members; wiring harnesses are protected within

E-Z-GO Textron WorkHorse 4x4 has an 800-pound payload, bucket seats, a forty-eight-inch bed with electric dump capacity, heavy-duty springs, and is a go-anywhere 4x4.

the frame. Electrically activated on-the-fly front or rear differential locks are easily selected with a dash-mounted rocker switch.

And yes, we drove this model into the same creek. Only this time Joan suggested I do the testing. We had no problem. Enclosed transmissions are also better when driving in high, wet grass, such as when getting to before-daylight turkey or deer hunting areas. Such conditions can also create problems with exposed belts. The unique center-mounted transmission does not protrude below the frame—nor does a short driveshaft. This offers greater protection for the drive train in rocky and stump-filled situations, as we discovered on a boulder-strewn trail. We also found that in four-wheel drive, the vehicle climbed up and over most of the logs blocking one trail. Steering is responsive and sure, as we learned on some winding trails with lots of sharp turns. There is, however, no engine braking for downhills.

An aggressive 9.5-inch ground clearance on the ST 4x4 provides go-anywhere capability for off-road use and protects the vehicle from the terrain. One feature I liked on the first model I tested, and retained on the new 4x4, is the self-cleaning, unidirectional 25-inch tires. The tire tread provides excellent traction in muddy, rocky, loose, or sandy surfaces.

The new 4x4 is powered by an 18-horsepower, 614cc, V-twin, air-cooled Honda engine. It will reach speeds up to 25 mph; response is quick both from the get-go and up through all the ranges. The key start and 340 CCA maintenance-free, vibration-resistant battery together provide quick and sure starts. A hinged front cowl allows easy access to the battery, the dual-circuit master cylinder, and the fuses.

The E-Z-GO is ruggedly built with a heavy-duty frame made of hot-dipped, galvanized channel and tubular steel throughout. This provides a very strong frame with corrosion protection. A roto-molded poly bed with no exposed hardware to rust or corrode adds to the rugged, long-lasting capabilities of the vehicle. You can haul manure, fertilizer, or a dead deer without worrying about corrosion. The new ST 4x4 has a big 1,100-pound bed load capacity and an impressive 1,500-pound vehicle load capacity. The bed has a manual, gas-assist lift with a removable fold-down tailgate that doesn't require a mechanical latch. I really like the way the bed is designed for hauling lots of different items. Four threaded inserts accept tiedowns. The bed measures 45 x 36 x 13.75 inches, and the 31-inch height makes loading heavy cargo easier. Molded-in slots allow you to section off the bed for different loads, to distribute the load weight, or keep items from shifting in rough country rides.

Seating consists of a thickly padded side-by-side bench for both driver and passenger. Dual-rate rear leaf springs add to the comfort, even in tough conditions. The dashboard, designed with convenient operation in mind, includes a passenger's-side storage tray with integral grab bar, two drink holders, a two-way radio or cell phone holder, and an optional 12-volt power outlet. Dash-mounted control knobs allow you to select front- or rear-locking differential and two- or four-wheel drive. The dashboard center gauge cluster includes an analog electric fuel gauge, analog voltmeter gauge, digital hour meter, parking brake indicator, low-oil indicator, front and rear differential lock indicator, and four-wheel-drive indicator.

Other standard features of the newer ST 4x4 include front hydraulic disc brakes and rear hydraulic drum brakes with all stainless-steel braided brake lines; dual halogen headlights; McPherson strut front suspension; rack-and-pinion steering; and a 2-inch front receiver that is compatible with a wide variety of hitches, winches, and aftermarket implements.

The E-Z-GO ST 4x4 has an automotive finish molded-in Recon Green front cowl and painted seat wrap. I found it an excellent, easy-driving vehicle with great off-road capability and plenty of hauling capacity.

Bad Boy Buggy

The Bad Boy Buggy indeed lives up to its name. This is the first-ever dual-motor, all-electric 4WD utility vehicle with reverse. Many of today's UTVs can trace their lineage back to electric golf carts, including the Bad Boy Buggy, but this machine takes the golf cart idea to the extreme. It's a muscle utility vehicle on steroids.

Actually, this was an unusual vehicle test. My first experience with the Bad Boy came during a dove hunt put on by the state of Mississippi, Mossy Oak, and Tufline ATV tools. The buggies were used to transport hunters on the Delta Ducks Plantation. I was so impressed with them, I made a point of getting hold of one for a short test period.

Bad Boy Buggy is a dual-motor, electric four-wheel UTV with reverse. An extremely powerful go-anywhere vehicle, it's also deadly quiet.

The Bad Boy Buggy comes with two 15.4-horsepower electric motors and is powered by eight 6-volt Trojan T-145 batteries; a 1,000-amp controller handles the torque of the two motors. Total horsepower is 31, delivering a hefty 170 foot-pounds of torque. You can travel up to 20 miles at up to 18 mph on a single charge. I used the vehicle all weekend and drew less than half a charge. A meter on the dash tells you the remaining power.

I assessed the vehicle on steep hills, down and through some rugged ravines, and into some fairly deep mud as well as some 12- to 18-inch water crossings. The mud-grip tires provided great traction even in the slick stuff. The vehicle bulled through all the obstacles with ease. The machine is amazingly fast on the top end, but can creep along like a silent turtle. Handling is straightforward, although the steering seemed a bit loose. The suspension leaves a bit to be desired, especially when moving along at top speed. The ride is fairly bouncy.

Braking was also a bit loose, although the parking brake is extremely effective and simple to use: Simply push the foot pedal all the way down to set it, or tap on the bottom edge of the pedal to release. The unit also has an electronic engine-braking feature. If you're going too fast downhill, push a button on the dash and get immediate braking. I welcomed this feature on one extremely steep hill with a sharp turn and drop-off. A push button on the dash also shifts into four-wheel, but I kept the vehicle on automatic four-wheel and it powered handily through everything.

The Bad Boy Buggy comes with a lift kit and 800-pound springs, providing a fairly high ground clearance, and an 800-pound load capacity. The vehicle is designed to be highly versatile. With the rear seat folded up, four people can ride, with the backseat facing rearward. A built-in rack is also available to hold tree stands or similar gear. The rear seat folds forward, providing a sturdy, smooth platform for toting gear or hauling out your game. A top with a sturdy roof rack can also carry a lot of gear such as lightweight tree stands.

Other standard features include a front bumper, front basket, windshield, headlights, auxiliary power, fender flares, and charger. The Bad Boy Buggy is available in various colors including Realtree Hardwoods and Mossy Oak Break-Up camo. An option is enclosing it completely for weather protection. The unit I tested had an optional gun rack. You can also add a winch fairly easily. A simple hitch is located on the rear, but given the torque these engines provide, I suggest a receiver hitch welded to the back instead of the pin hitch. This would allow for more uses, such as pulling food-plot tools. A large glove box is located on either side of the dash, and a four-cup holder is located in its front edge.

The main feature for hunting, however, is no noise. I drove up on numerous deer and turkeys during my weekend of testing. *Note:* Most states do not allow hunting from a vehicle, which would include a utility vehicle. And, of course, it's morally wrong. Still, this vehicle lets you slip in and out of the stand or blind in your favorite hunting spot without undue spooking of game. This can help prevent game patterning your route or time of travel. For scouting or simply observing wildlife, this machine is a great deal of fun.

The Bad Boy Buggy is sturdy and versatile enough for farm and other work, and it's quiet enough to make it suitable for around-the-house gardening and landscaping chores as well as for transporting hunters, gear, and game. It's a great all-purpose vehicle.

Club Car Pioneer 1200

Club Car, the world's leading manufacturer of golf carts, also carries a Pioneer line of Performance Utility Vehicles. Designed to handle a wide variety of uses, the Club Car Pioneer is the first in a new generation of rough-terrain utility vehicles offering superior operation, versatility, and a comfortable ride. Pioneer is made with the same unequaled quality and dependability as the entire family of Club Car vehicles.

Available in two models, the durable and reliable Pioneer line offers up to 15.3 cubic feet of cargo volume, 6.6 and 6.4 inches of ground clearance, and a top speed of 19 mph, making it one of the most adaptable utility vehicles available. Club Car's 1200 and 900 utility vehicles come with a two-year limited warranty, the longest available in the industry.

Farmers and ranchers will find the new Pioneer machines valuable for their power and hauling capacity, making it easy to cross rough terrain, climb hills, and carry heavy loads. The Pioneer offers reliable versatility on construction sites, where its tight turning radius allows it to haul lumber or tow a trailer through areas a pickup can't traverse. Sportsmen will appreciate the Pioneer's smooth ride, comfortable and spacious seating, and standard cargo box.

The Club Car Pioneer utility vehicles are available in two models with up to 15.3 cubic feet of cargo volume, off-road styling, and bucket seats. (Photo courtesy Club Car)

The Pioneer 1200 features off-road styling and bucket seats as well as a key-start 351cc, 11-horsepower gasoline engine with a total vehicle load capacity of 1,200 pounds; shift-on-the-fly operator-selected differential lock; independent front suspension with coil-over shocks and semi-independent rear suspension with multileaf springs and dual hydraulic brakes; a rustproof, corrosion-resistant aluminum I-beam chassis; four-wheel hydraulic drum brakes; 2-inch front and rear receiver hitch; and all-terrain mud or turf tires. The Pioneer 900 features traditional styling and bench seats, as well as a key-start 351cc, 11-horsepower gasoline engine, with a total vehicle load capacity of 900 pounds.

Cub Cadet Big Country 4x2
Known for quality lawn and garden equipment for more than 40 years, Cub Cadet entered the hunting and outdoor utility vehicle market with two machines. The first was a 6x4 vehicle; 2004 saw the introduction of a more agile, maneuverable 4x2 model for the hunting and outdoor market. Both now feature Mossy Oak camouflage.

Cub Cadet Big Country 4x2 is an agile, easily maneuvered UTV featuring 2WD with a differential lock for 4WD. Shifting is electric with a push button on the dash.

The 4x2 features an 18-horsepower Honda V-twin OHV engine. It has a standard CVT (continuously variable transmission) running 2WD, with a differential lock for 4WD. The belt drive is exposed, which means this is not a "wet" machine. It's not made for deep creek crossings or mud runs. The transaxle, however, is fully enclosed, oil-bath lubricated. On the other hand, speeds are infinitely variable up to 19 mph.

The first thing you notice about the vehicle is that there's no gearshift. Shifting is as easy as pushing a button on the dash, which takes some getting used to—but then it's "Hey, that's great." The brake has to be fully on for the engine to start and to shift. Then you push a button for reverse, forward, or neutral. If the button-controlled shift malfunctions, you can reach under the seat and manually move the shift lever. I did not, however, have any problems. In fact, shifting couldn't be simpler. A lighted dash cluster indicates the gear position. Unfortunately, a beeper comes on when you shift into reverse—a definite irritation in the deer woods. A dash-mounted push button shifts the differential lock in and out, again very simple.

The next thing you notice in examining the machine is its sturdiness. The all-welded steel frame comes from experience in building hardworking machines.

The Cub Cadet performed beautifully in my tests. Riding is comfortable in well-padded bucket seats with two molded-in cup holders as well as a small accessory box for items such as keys or small tools. The driver's seat is adjustable front to back, making it easy to fit different statures. The seats fold forward; the driver's seat has the 5.7-gallon fuel tank with a fuel gauge on the top. A low-fuel warning light is also located on the dash. A big, easy-to-get-to gas fill tube is located on the side of the passenger's-seat box. The passenger's side has a large underseat storage box for tools or supplies. In addition, a roomy, but open, glove box is located in the dash. The underseat storage, cup holders, and glove box all have drainholes to allow rainwater to escape. A 12-volt dash-mounted plug is standard equipment. An automotive-style fuse block is located under the front cowling. The area under the front cowling is easily accessed by removing a pair of thumb toggles.

The ride was fairly soft, but still with a good bounce. The suspension features fully independent A-arms with coils over shocks in the front, and semi-independent leaf springs with hydraulic shocks in the rear. Steering was a breeze due to the rack-and-pinion system with its Ackerman-type geometry. Turning radius, however, is a bit big at 21 feet. Braking is with a 7-inch self-adjusting drum located in the rear. Parking is achieved by pushing in the foot brake pedal and pulling out a dash-mounted lever. The unit I tested also came with a front brushguard and rubber floor mat. Big, sturdy handholds are located on both sides of the seats. This is especially appreciated by passengers. Dual 37.5-watt halogen lights provide plenty of nighttime illumination. The high-impact Mossy Oak body panels are made to resist cracking and scratching to help keep the machine looking new.

The bed capacity is 11.3 cubic feet with an 800-pound load capacity. Total capacity is 1,200 pounds, which includes a 200-pound operator and 200-pound passenger along with maximum bed capacity. The bed is 14-gauge steel and is rubber isolated. Again, this is a sturdy, well-built vehicle made to haul and work. The bed sides have slots in them, making it easy to use tiedowns or even add stake sides to add bed height. An convenient latch next to the driver and sturdy handles on each side make it easy to utilize the dump bed. The one option I would install is an electric bed lift. The vehicle comes with the option of turf or trail tires; the unit I tested had trail tires. The overall design of the vehicle creates an extremely low-center-of-gravity machine. A Class I receiver hitch comes standard on the model I tested.

The Cub Cadet Camo Big Country 4x2 is a well-built, easy-riding, easy-driving, and easy-handling utility vehicle that will work hard, and then play hard when you want to hit the woods.

ARGO 8x8 Conquest

"Get in," said Gene Lintz, an ARGO dealer from Crawfordsville, Iowa, as he ran the unusual-looking vehicle off the ramp in my driveway. I directed him to a road through our timberland; before I could even get seated we were off and speeding along the twisting road. "Works like this," he said and immediately turned the vehicle on its own axis. Before I could catch my breath we were speeding back in the opposite direction. "Have fun," Gene laughed as he drove off, leaving the vehicle for me to play with. And I did.

The Argo 8x8 Conquest is literally a go-anywhere vehicle, on land or water, driven by a variable speed transmission and six wheels. Steering is by two levers.

My wife, Joan, and I tested the vehicle that evening and the next morning, before Gene came back to pick it up. I never got quite as good at driving the vehicle as the dealer; it does take some learning and practice to drive. The vehicle is steered by two movable handlebars, with the throttle control on the right one. Twisting the grip opens the throttle. The belt-driven Continuously Variable Transmission (CVT) maximizes engine power to the transmission with high and low ranges forward, along with neutral and reverse. All this is compactly housed in a very efficient planetary differential. Pulling back on one lever applies the hydraulic brakes to the wheels on that side. Pulling back on both levers applies brakes to stop the vehicle—and it really stops fast.

Front and rear axle bearing extensions provide increased axle and bearing life. For safety and ease of handling, the ARGO steering transmission provides continuous torque to all axles; never does one wheel grab. The machine will literally turn on its center axis, and is nimble and fun to drive once you master the technique. The ARGO 8x8 Conquest is also extremely powerful, thanks to a 617cc Kawasaki engine. Top speed on land is a pretty fast and bouncy 20 mph. Speed on water is 2.5 mph. Steering and propulsion on water are basically the same as on land. The special lugged tires provide the propulsion; you steer by stopping the wheels on one side. Water turns were much larger in radius than the land turns, and the machine doesn't stop very fast in the water.

Joan and I took the Conquest to the creek on our property, where I made a serious mistake. With no fear, I drove the vehicle into the creek, only to immediately high center it on a big rock. During another test, Joan drowned a vehicle in the creek when she accidentally got too deep. I had to wade out, attach a winch, and use another vehicle to extract her. With the ARGO balanced perfectly on the rock, it was déjà vu. Joan laughingly suggested that I start taking off my boots, but with a little powering back and forth, the vehicle slid off. It comes with a full skid plate, so the underside wasn't damaged. After my initial mistake, the Conquest simply went where I pointed it, when I managed to steer it properly.

Through a marsh, up and over steep creekbanks, climbing over logs in a logging slash pile, and finally a test in the pond below the house proved that the ARGO 8x8 Conquest is a true go-anywhere vehicle. Although it sits slightly forward on the water, there was no tippiness during the ride, or even when I stood up to make a few casts. It is suggested that you not stand up in the unit while in the water. All riders must wear an approved PFD when on the water in the vehicle. It is also suggested a helmet and eye protection be worn during on-land use.

Seating consists of a very comfortable front bench seat with a padded backrest. There's plenty of room for two adults on the seat, with room for the driver to steer and drive quite easily. The rear compartment has two narrow but comfortably padded bench seats, one on each side. The Conquest 8x8 will seat six people on land, four on water.

The 8x8 Conquest will also haul a pretty heavy load, with a rating of 1,000 pounds. The cargo area has a removable floor that allows you to get at the drive chains if necessary, but also makes it easy to clean out the unit when it becomes muddy. The cargo area is quite deep and will hold a passel of things such as goose decoys. In fact, I would really have liked to test the unit during goose season. Missouri "gumbo" mud, found in the best goose fields, is a test for any vehicle. And with a tow rating of 1,600 pounds, you can tow just about anything you can hook to it. These ratings are suggestions from the manufacturer and are approximate. Safe towing and loading depends on the type of surface and the load as well as the incline.

There just about isn't any job the Conquest won't handle—bogs, marshes, dense undergrowth, up and over hills, across ponds and rivers. And the low-ground-pressure tires don't damage fragile environments, if the vehicle is driven sensibly. ARGOs are being used for many agricultural and forestry uses, such as transporting firewood, hauling trailers, firefighting, plowing snow, making maple syrup, and hauling people. Because they're truly amphibious, the all-terrain capability also makes them popular with disaster response, search-and-rescue, emergency medical, and geological surveying teams, among other chores. If you're a hunter, angler, or outdoor enthusiast, you'll find lots of work and play for the 8x8 Conquest. Ice fishers have found that ARGO vehicles are a safer way to go, transversing the ice handily and floating should you break through. The special webbed tires actually work as linear propellers in the water.

Standard features include a voltmeter, hour meter, temperature gauge, low-charge-rate light, and low-oil-pressure light. To lock the unit in park, parking brakes are simple levers located on each steering handlebar. Removable plugs are located in the bottom of the unit at the back for draining out water.

After testing and examining the ARGO 8x8 Conquest, I'm convinced that it's a well-made and sturdy machine. The frame is made of formed steel channel, welded for high strength and durability. It is polyester powder coated for lasting protection. The body is vacuum formed of high density polyethylene (HDPE). A see-through fuel tank with easily reached exterior fill tube makes it simple to determine gasoline quantity as well as to fill. The ground pressure is only 3 to 4 psi with wheels and less than 1 psi with tracks. And if you have a flat tire, you're not stranded. ARGOs are manufactured by Ontario Drive & Gear Limited in Ontario, Canada, well-known for their high-quality products. Actually, four ARGO models are produced: the 6x6 Bigfoot, 6x6 Conquest, 8x8 Response, and 8x8 Conquest. ARGO also produces the Centaur, a more powerful version used primarily for commercial work.

A number of accessories are available, including windscreens; brushguard kit; heater kit; roll-over protection structure (ROPS); rear bench seat kit, with seat belts; roll bar light kit; cargo tiedown kit; tow hook kit, for front or rear; utility storage pouch; bilge pump kit (recommended for amphibious use by any ARGO, this is operated by a dash-mounted switch to quickly remove water from the lower body); cloth covers; winches; snowplows; dump beds; cargo racks; and even a four-wheeled amphibious trailer. An outboard motor bracket accepts electric or gasoline motors up to 9.9 hp.

For serious or extended water use, this is the best choice. With a side-mounted outboard motor mount, the amphibious trailer can be towed in the water as well. Just think about all the decoys you could tote. Tracks make the vehicle even better in snow or mud, and three different track kits are available—standard, supertrack, and a version for the ice. ARGO units are available in several colors as well as Bill Jordan's Advantage Wetlands camouflage design.

If you have challenging terrain, the amphibian ARGO 8x8 Conquest is more than capable . . . a real go-anywhere vehicle.

BUYING A UTILITY VEHICLE

As with purchasing any ATV, it's important to deal with a reputable local dealer. And as these vehicles have become more and more popular, the number of dealerships throughout the country has grown greatly.

Before buying, carefully consider the uses of the vehicle. For instance, if you will be using it for tilling food plots, you'll need one of the heavier, more powerful models. If, on the other hand, you'll be taking stands and hunters to the woods in pursuit of deer, a smaller model is more maneuverable. Waterfowl hunters who need to traverse wetlands, ricefields, and similar areas will find four-wheel drive a necessity. If you need to transport the vehicle to your hunting or fishing area, a model that fits in a pickup bed may be your best choice.

Most vehicle manufacturers and some accessory companies offer aftermarket accessories to make these machines even more versatile. You also may wish to check out the accessories to determine the models that best suit your needs. Chapter 9 details the products currently on the market.

3

Safety

The popularity of ATVs is growing by leaps and bounds—and naturally this increases the chances for accidents. As with any motorized vehicle, specific safety rules must be followed when using ATVs. Research indicates that major factors in ATV-associated injuries are rider misuse and inappropriate rider behavior, including riding without a helmet, riding double, riding on paved surfaces, riding while under the influence of alcohol or drugs, and other risky conduct in violation of the distributors' warnings.

With the increasing popularity of ATVs comes more need for learning and following ATV safety rules. (Photo courtesy Honda)

OWNER'S MANUALS

The first step in safety is to read and understand the owner's manual and warning labels on your ATV. Different models handle and react differently in different situations. Make sure you thoroughly read the owner's manual and understand how your particular ATV must be ridden.

CHILDREN AND ATVS

A major problem arises when children are permitted to operate adult-sized ATVs. Every adult-sized ATV has a permanently affixed label warning that children under age 16 should "never operate" the ATV because they face increased risk of "severe injury or death." The same warnings are repeated at the dealer showroom and in the owner's manual.

Youth-model ATVs of 90ccs or less are available for children age 12 or older and are to be ridden under adult supervision.

ATVs carry warning labels of specific safety rules.

These vehicles are smaller, lighter, and slower than adult models. Youth models also come with throttle limiters that allow parents to control vehicle speeds. Even with these safety features, the ATV industry warns parents and other adults to supervise young operators at all times. ATVs are not toys. They are motorized vehicles that require close parental supervision. With proper supervision, youth-model vehicles provide a safe and important alternative for children 12 and older.

Safe Riding Education

As ATV sales grew steadily into the early 1980s, American Honda and other manufacturers and distributors of ATVs—including Yamaha Motor Corporation, USA; American Suzuki Motor Corporation; and Kawasaki Motors Corporation, USA—formed the Specialty Vehicle Institute of America (SVIA) in 1983. This Irvine, California–based nonprofit was created to provide information on ATV standards as well as to promote model state legislation on ATV riding. Learning from its successful sister organization, the Motorcycle Safety Foundation (founded in 1972), the SVIA created its own all-terrain vehicle training program. Formed to promote the safe and responsible use of ATVs, the SVIA soon established the nonprofit ATV Safety Institute (ASI) to implement a national program of ATV safety education, awareness, and training.

ATV RiderCourse

The ASI targets ATV users and potential buyers with highly visible messages about the safe and responsible use of ATVs. A significant part of this effort is a hands-on training program called the ATV RiderCourse. This half-day course provides an opportunity to increase riders' safety knowledge and to practice basic riding skills in a controlled environment under the direct supervision of a certified instructor. Students practice safety techniques with hands-on exercises covering starting and stopping, turning, negotiating hills, emergency stopping and swerving, and riding over obstacles. Particular emphasis is placed on the safety implications relating to each lesson. The course also covers protective gear, environmental concerns, and local laws.

Taking an ATV course is a first step in learning proper and safe use of the vehicle. (Photo courtesy Yamaha)

More than 700 active instructors are certified to teach the ASI ATV RiderCourse at more than 1,000 locations throughout all 50 states. Using a curriculum designed in consultation with the Consumer Product Safety Commission (CPSC), the course is free to individual purchasers and their immediate family members, and to other interested parties for a modest fee.

Special provisions are made for students under 16, and parents are encouraged to attend the class as well. Students under 12 participate in a separate class, but parents must be present during the entire course. Children as young as six may take the class using appropriately sized machines.

The nationwide ASI program has trained more than 330,000 ATV riders since 1988, including more than 45,500 first-time purchasers and family members. The success of this training program is unprecedented in any industry.

Honda's dedication to its customers' safety goes beyond the industry-sponsored programs. The firm has four Rider Education Centers in key regions of the United States, staffed and maintained by American Honda since the late 1980s. The company invested $10 million to build these state-of-the-art training facilities for ATV riders, as well as riders of street and off-road motorcycles. Significantly, these sites are open to riders of all brands to participate in state- and industry-sponsored training.

National 4-H Council

While manufacturers and the Consumer Product Safety Commission strongly discourage the use of ATVs by those 16 or younger, it was inevitable that younger riders were operating ATVs in farming environments that included tractors and other machinery. This situation grew particularly clear to the National 4-H Council, an institution with strong ties to America's rural communities and farms. Agencies observed that, in many cases, farm families were confused by the contradiction that their young teens could operate powerful and expensive farm equipment under the watchful eye of an adult, yet were considered too young to operate an adult-sized ATV with an engine size greater than 90cc.

Pursuing its mission to promote youth education, the National 4-H Council approached American Honda with the intention of developing an ATV education program addressing these concerns. With the concurrence of the CPSC and the financial support of American Honda, the 4-H created the 4-H ATV Community Safety Education Program.

A key component of this ongoing program is 4-H's ATV Fit Guidelines, which stress the need for a young ATV operator to possess the mental and emotional maturity necessary to operate a motorized vehicle, adding that a parent or guardian is best equipped to make this decision. Once this baseline is established, simple physical sizing guidelines are provided that properly fit a young person to an appropriately sized ATV. While it is plausible that a 14-year-old may have the maturity and physical size to operate an adult-sized ATV, it is equally possible that a 17-year-old may not.

4-H and Honda have helped create classroom curriculums concerning ATV use and youth. (Photo courtesy Honda)

With the help of American Honda, the 4-H developed a classroom curriculum designed to spread the message through schools in communities where ATVs are popular. Organized by state 4-H Extension offices, the programs are taught by 4-H agents and other community volunteers. The 4-H Council estimates that tens of millions of safety awareness impressions have been created since the program's inception in July 1989. Honda continues to fund this important project.

"Ride Smart, Stupid Hurts"

To further promote the responsible use of ATVs, American Honda launched a nationwide public awareness campaign in September 1998 called "Ride Smart, Stupid Hurts." The innovative program delivers straightforward messages encouraging free ATV rider training, helmet use, operator-only use, drug- and alcohol-free operation, appropriate age/vehicle size, youth supervision, and off-highway-only use. Each topic strongly encourages parents and adults to act responsibly with youths riding ATVs. The slogan "Stupid Hurts" is intended to create a lasting impression on parents and youngsters who read or view the campaign materials.

Print advertising of the Honda's campaign encouraged readers to order a free safety information kit by calling 800-905-5565. Readers received an introductory letter, a Honda "Ride Smart" riding tips guide, and several "Stupid Hurts" stickers printed on an adhesive bandage design.

The "Ride Smart, Stupid Hurts" message is also incorporated as a central theme in Honda's safety awareness video, *FourTrax, Play It Smart*, which is provided free to all purchasers of new Honda ATVs.

SAFETY BASICS

Gear and Clothing

The single most important piece of protective gear is the helmet. While color, design, and price may influence the helmet-purchase decision, protection must be the first consideration. The full-faced helmet clearly provides the most protection, but it must fit properly in order to do its job. A helmet should fit snugly but comfortably, and be securely fastened. Hockey, football, or skateboard helmets

The first step in safe use is always to wear a helmet and eye protection.

Protective clothing should also be worn, including appropriate over-the-ankle boots. (Photo courtesy Suzuki)

are not acceptable for ATV riding, as they do not have adequate safety features for use while operating a motorized vehicle. Eye protection in the form of goggles or a face shield is also extremely important.

Other protective clothing includes off-road-style, or leather, gloves; shoulder pads/chest protector for off-road enthusiasts; off-road pants with knee and shin pads; and over-the-ankle ATV boots (although most hunters will probably wear their hunting boots). During winter, it's important to wear clothing that keeps you dry and warm. You can easily become chilled while riding an ATV. Clothing should be snug, but loose enough to permit freedom of movement and good blood circulation.

Hunting Safety

In addition to wearing the proper clothing, matching the vehicle to the rider, and understanding safe operation of the particular ATV, hunters and shooters must know and follow other safety rules. All guns must be unloaded and strapped in gun racks or gun boots made specifically for holding firearms on ATVs. In many instances,

Hunters using ATVs should also follow safe hunting rules, including unloading guns for transport and safely securing them to the vehicle. (Photo courtesy Arctic Cat)

Extra care should be taken when ATVs are used for pulling ground working equipment. Do not exceed the manufacturer's tow rating.

hunters also use ATVs for hauling or dragging deer and other big game from the woods. Do not exceed the capacity rating of the ATV racks. Make sure the carcass is well secured. Be particularly cautious in traversing sidehills, as the weight of the animal can tip the ATV over. If you're dragging a big-game carcass, downed tree for

Don't overload the racks of the ATV. Be especially careful with water-filled tanks and other heavy equipment that can shift and create an imbalance.

the campfire, or other heavy object, take extra care not to allow the vehicle to tip over backward. Be extra careful when sidehilling, too, because the object may roll downhill and tip the ATV over.

Pulling Safety

ATVs are often used to pull groundbreaking or other heavy equipment. Again, extra care must be taken so as not to tip over the vehicle. Do not exceed the manufacturer's tow rating. Some riders disdain helmets for this slow work, but that's a serious mistake.

Overloading the racks can also create problems. If you secure a water or chemical tank onto your ATV rack, for example, the extra weight can seriously imbalance the vehicle. A friend once endured several hours pinned under his ATV due to a moment of carelessness while using a loaded farm chemical sprayer attached to a rack on his bike. His kids finally came looking for him and pulled the vehicle off. He was, needless to say, extremely lucky to walk away from the accident unharmed.

Transporting ATVs

Loading and unloading ATVs onto a truck or trailer for transportation also requires considerations for safety. Chapter 11 contains information on loading, unloading, transporting ATVs.

Safety Information

The ATV Safety Institute offers two free brochures: *Tips and Practice Guide for the ATV Rider* and *Parents, Youngsters and ATVs*. It also has a video, *Riding Tips for ATV Riders*, available for consumer viewing at ATV dealerships. The video can be borrowed from dealerships or purchased from ASI. Call the ATV safety hotline at 800-852-5344 to learn more. Additional safety information is available in your owner's manuals.

By following proper safety rules, you'll find that ATVs can add to the enjoyment and productiveness of hunting and other outdoor activities. They can also open up a whole new way of enjoying the great outdoors.

Riding Techniques

Riding ATVs is fun—it's that simple. Like many other activities, however, ATV riding must be properly learned. Many first-time buyers or riders simply get on and head for the off-road country. That can be a serious mistake. Improper use of ATVs can result in serious injury or death.

Riding ATVs is fun, but is a skill that must be properly learned, like riding a bicycle or driving an automobile. (Photo courtesy Honda)

ATVs don't drive like automobiles (except for the utility vehicles). They don't handle or drive like motorcycles or bicycles, either. They require different driving and handling skills, and it's important that riders learn and practice them.

Beginning riders should practice starting the vehicle, driving, braking, and turning in an open, off-road area, away from other riders. The terrain should be flat and free of obstacles, and have either a loose or hard dirt surface, not a mixture of both. Do not ride on pavement—ATVs are not designed for pavement. The *Tips and Practice Guide for the ATV Rider* booklet from the ATV Safety Institute describes how to set up a learning course, with tips for mastering the basics.

Most ATVs are designed to carry only one person. An ATV does not have a seat strap, dual seat, passenger's grab rail, or foot pegs for a passenger. The long seat is needed for the operator in order to maintain vehicle control by shifting body weight. A passenger interferes with the operator's ability to control the vehicle. Also, a passenger impairs the steering response of the vehicle by shifting

Most ATVs are designed to carry only one person. A passenger can interfere with the operator's ability to control the vehicle by shifting body weight.

Some ATVs now are designed to carry two persons.

weight from the front wheels, causing loss of control, which may result in an accident. And without secure seating, a passenger may lose his or her balance and fall off the vehicle. Some longer-wheelbase ATVs, however, are now available for two riders.

Plain old common sense goes a long way in preventing accidents and adds to the pleasure of ATV riding.

- Don't try wheelies and jumps.
- Don't ride at excessive speeds, or too fast for the conditions or your skill level.
- Never drink and drive. Alcohol and drugs impair your judgment and slow your reactions. Even prescription drugs can be dangerous. If you take prescription drugs, check with your doctor before riding.
- Always ride with both feet on the footboards. If you have experience riding a motorcycle, this step may be hard to unlearn. Removing a foot from the footboard can cause you to lose your balance, and your foot may be caught by the rear wheel and cause an accident.
- Keep both hands on the handlebars.

- Before starting the engine, set the parking brake; place the transmission in neutral (many ATVs will start while in gear, so make sure the brake is on before starting); and check the throttle to make sure it is operating properly. It should snap back closed when released.
- When you're getting off the ATV, always apply the parking brake to keep the vehicle from rolling or moving.

MODIFICATIONS AND ACCESSORIES

Any modifications to a factory vehicle, or the addition of accessories, can change the handling of the ATV. Make sure all accessories are properly installed, and follow the loading information in the owner's manual.

If you're towing, follow only the specified tongue weight as per the manufacturer's specifications.

Make sure you follow all safety checks before riding, including inspecting tire pressure as specified by the manufacturer.

It's important to maintain correct posture in order to control the vehicle by shifting your body weight. (Photo courtesy Yamaha)

POSTURE

Because ATVs are rider-active, the correct posture makes riding easier and safer. This lets you shift your body weight as needed for maneuvering. Riding can be done sitting or standing, depending on the situation. Keep your head and eyes up and focus on the riding path and terrain. Your shoulders should be relaxed, elbows bent slightly out and away from your body. Both hands should be on the handlebars and both feet should be on the footrests, toes pointing straight ahead. Your knees should be in toward the gas tank. If you're standing, keep your knees bent slightly to help absorb the movement from riding.

SHIFTING GEARS

ATVs have different types of transmissions. Make sure you read the owner's manual and understand how to operate the transmission on the model you are riding. Always close the throttle while shifting to prevent the front wheels from lifting. If your ATV has a manual clutch, learn where the engagement zone is to prevent stalling and to allow for smooth operation of the vehicle. The majority of today's ATVs are automatic, using a slip-torque drive belt. These are the easiest to drive.

BRAKING

Read your owner's manual to understand what types of brakes your ATV has. These may be separate front and rear brakes, or a rear brake only, or in some cases one brake control for all four wheels. If dual brakes are available, use both equally. Avoid sudden braking of the front wheels, which can cause a dangerous situation and possibly flip the ATV or throw you from it. Do not apply excessive braking while cornering. If you're descending a long hill, use a lower gear and avoid excessive braking.

In the case of four-wheel-drive modes, using only the front or only the rear brake has the effect of braking both the front and rear wheels. Sudden deceleration by shifting to a lower gear, or releasing the throttle on engines equipped with engine-braking features, will also affect both the front and rear wheels on four-wheel-drive vehicles.

OBSTACLES

Before riding in an area you are unfamiliar with, check it out for hidden dangers or obstacles. Keep your speed down until you know the area. A friend was thrown entirely over the handlebars of his ATV while riding too fast through a mud hole. An unseen rut literally stopped the ATV in its tracks. Luckily, he was uninjured, although he did manage to snap the steering column.

Use existing trails and avoid unsafe areas such as extremely rough, slippery, or loose terrain. Don't attempt to ride over large obstacles. When riding over small obstacles, approach slowly. As the vehicle goes up and over, shift your weight to stay centered. Stand up if necessary to maintain your balance, and use careful throttle control. You can easily tip an ATV over backward with too much power—or you may suddenly clear the obstacle, only to have your body thrown forward.

Stay alert to terrain changes, downhill and uphill slopes, twists, turns with side slopes, and other dangerous areas.

Be aware of obstacles. Check for them before riding in an unfamiliar area, or off trails.

RIDING IN REVERSE

Do not ride in reverse except at low speed. Make sure you look behind you before proceeding in reverse.

MAKING TURNS

Learn to make turns at slow speeds in a large, open area. Use the throttle to maintain an even speed through the turn. Since both rear wheels of an ATV turn at the same speed, the inside wheel gives up traction or "slips" on the ground during the turn. Sliding forward in the seat and leaning to the inside of the turn help the rear wheels turn easier and improve front-wheel steering. As you turn more sharply or increase speed, move forward and lean to the inside of the turn. If the vehicle begins to tip during the turn, lean your body even farther into the turn and reduce the throttle. Don't put a foot down on the ground; maintain both feet on the footboards.

To make turns, slide forward in the seat and lean to the inside of the turn—but keep both feet on the floor boards. (Photo courtesy Suzuki)

There is also a great deal of difference in steering between 2WD and 4WD modes. With two-wheel you can begin the turn, add just a bit more throttle, and "slide" the rear wheels slightly to assist in the turn. This takes a bit of getting used to and shouldn't be overdone when first learning. This method is not effective in 4WD mode because all four wheels have power.

The type of terrain has a great deal of effect on turning. Loose material allows the rear wheels to slip easily, and the vehicle tends to turn more sharply. Harder surfaces do not allow the rear wheels to slip as readily, causing the turning radius to increase. This means you must allow more room to complete the turn.

HILL CLIMBING

Hill climbing is a lot of fun. Do not, however, climb hills until you have learned the proper methods of driving on relatively flat surfaces. Then begin on gentle slopes and gradually increase the incline. Do not attempt hills that are too steep for the ATV or your abilities.

When climbing hills, lean forward to keep weight forward. On steep hills you may need to stand and lean forward.

Lean forward while climbing to keep the front wheels from lifting. On steeper hills, you may need to stand and lean forward for more weight transfer. The front wheels must be kept on the ground so you can steer, and also to prevent the possibility of tipping over backward.

When approaching a hill, select low gears to reach the top without losing momentum. Speed up before ascending to gain momentum. Don't apply power suddenly or change gears while climbing; this may cause the front wheels to come off the ground, and the vehicle could flip over backward.

Do not go over a hill at high speed. An obstacle, a sharp drop, or another vehicle or person could be on the other side. If you can't see over the hill, slow down until you can get a clear view. Do not climb hills where you cannot see far enough ahead, and avoid those with slippery surfaces that will cause you to lose traction.

If the vehicle doesn't have enough power to reach the top of the hill and starts to lose momentum, turn around and ride downhill if you have enough space. Be extra careful on the turn not to tip the vehicle over sideways. Keep your weight on the uphill side during the turn.

If the vehicle stalls on a hill, apply the brakes before the unit starts to roll backward. If it should start to roll back, apply the brakes gradually. You may tip the vehicle over if you apply either the front or rear brakes suddenly, or if you try to apply power while rolling backward. If you are stopped on a hillside, apply the parking brake and carefully dismount on the uphill side of the vehicle (so it cannot roll over on you). To turn the machine around, drag the rear end of the ATV uphill as far as possible. Remount from the uphill side if it is not facing straight downhill. Then, while keeping as much of your weight as possible on the uphill side, turn the handlebar downhill. Release the parking brake and, in low gear, ride downhill.

DOWNHILLING

Downhilling is often scarier than uphilling to beginning riders, especially if the slope is steep and comes as a surprise. Make sure you slow or stop at the top of a hill so you can determine a safe path where you can see far enough ahead to avoid any obstacles. Choose low gear for descending. If possible, you should descend in a straight path downward. Riding at an angle can cause the vehicle

When descending hills, slow down or stop at the top to determine a safe path down. Shift into low gear and lean backward.

to lean to one side and possibly tip over. Sit back in the seat and brace yourself by straightening your arms. Hold your speed down by keeping the throttle closed. If the ATV is equipped with engine braking, this can also be an assist, as the torque of the engine will help to slow the vehicle.

Brake as necessary, applying both front and rear brakes gradually. Avoid the sudden application of either the front or rear brakes, which can cause the vehicle to overturn. Be especially careful if the surface is loose; the tires may skid, and braking effectiveness may be reduced.

Turning while descending a slope must be done carefully and gradually to avoid tipping the vehicle over. Keep your feet on the floorboards and transfer your weight to the rear and uphill side of the vehicle.

SIDEHILLING

Sidehilling can be especially dangerous because the machine can tip over. Keep your body weight toward the top of the hill. Avoid

Sidehilling can be dangerous because the vehicle can tip over. Keep your weight toward the uphill side.

hills with slippery surfaces that can cause you to lose traction. Also avoid traversing hillsides covered with rocks and other obstacles, which may cause you to lose your balance and tip over.

If the vehicle begins to tip, steer downhill if possible to regain control. If you discover that the vehicle is in danger of rolling over, dismount on the uphill side. *Hint:* In hilly country, use an antenna flag so others can see you coming from the other side of the hill or sand dune. Take extra care when approaching blind hilltops and corners.

RIDING IN WATER AND MUD

Water crossings and mud holes can be fun. They can also be deadly at the worst or, at the least, just plain embarrassing. The first step is to assess the situation. Water and mud can conceal many hazards. Check the water before entering for rocks, holes, and other obstacles that may cause you to overturn or become stuck or submerged. Choose a location to enter and exit the water where the banks are not too steep or slippery.

Also watch for excess current. Do not attempt to cross streams or rivers with swiftly flowing water. If the vehicle loses traction, it could be swept into the current. If you're crossing a stream with moderate current, enter the water upstream of where you intend to make your landing.

Never operate an ATV in deep water. The maximum safe riding depth is up to the bottom edge of the axle caps in quiet, slow-moving water. Vehicle operation in deep water may be unpredictable and hazardous. On a water crossing on Alaska's Kodiak Island, one vehicle was swept off its wheels completely, overturned in the river, and then swept downstream as it turned over and over. The rider safely got off the vehicle before it turned over.

Riding in mud requires the same careful attention to the path—looking for unseen obstacles. Mud can also be extremely slippery, creating steering problems. And hidden ruts can also cause sudden steering problems. Footrests may become slippery in mud and water.

Driving ATVs in muddy conditions takes practice. If you must cross fairly long expanses of mud, keep up a steady speed to maintain headway. In order to not get bogged down, preselect your route if possible, then maintain enough power to drive through the

Do not operate an ATV in deep or swift water. Operating depth is up to the bottom edge of the axle cap.

Mud can hide obstacles and create unsafe situations. Take it slow and easy until you determine what's hidden.

mud. This is where practice comes in. Too little power and the ATV tends to settle in the mud. Too much and the tires can dig a hole before you can react.

After riding your ATV in water or mud, test the brakes. Some exposed belt systems may slip. To dry out the belts, shift the engine into neutral and apply full throttle for about 10 seconds. Allow the

Thoroughly check your ATV before beginning a trail ride to make sure there are no maintenance problems.

engine to come back to idle and repeat as needed. Make sure to conduct proper maintenance, as covered in Chapter 10, after riding in these adverse conditions.

SAND

Riding sand dunes is great recreation in areas where they're available. Always use an antenna flag on your ATV to increase your visibility to other drivers. Be prepared for changing sand conditions and avoid wet sand. Be aware of overhangs or slip faces and razorbacks. Be especially careful when the sun is directly overhead—the lack of shadows can make it difficult to see hazards.

After riding in sand, make sure you check and clean your air filter.

SNOW

Riding on snow can be a great deal of fun, but it can also be dangerous. Firm snow, without ice, usually causes the fewest problems. Soft snow can hide dangerous obstacles, and it makes sense to stay on firm snow or groomed ATV trails when possible. If you're using snowmobile trails, check with local authorities to determine if ATVs are allowed.

Ice can cause serious problems. If possible, avoid excessively slippery areas. Regardless, slow down when encountering slippery areas such as wet snow or ice, and use extra caution. Maintain a high level of alertness, reading the trail and avoiding quick, sharp turns, which can cause skids. Do not apply brakes during a skid; you can lose control. If the ATV begins to skid, turn the handlebars in the direction of the skid and shift your body weight forward. If your machine has four-wheel drive, use it to assist in control in slippery areas.

In addition to pleasure riding or using an ATV for wintertime hunting, camping, and fishing activities (they're great for hauling ice-fishing gear onto a frozen lake), with the right accessories ATVs can also be used to move snow. Snow blades, snowplows, and even snow throwers are available to fit most of the larger, utility-sized ATVs.

Hunting with ATVs and Utility Vehicles

The late Ben Lee, one of the best pro hunters of modern times, was one of the first outdoorsmen to appreciate the use of a four-wheeler for hunting. His four-wheeler went with him everywhere he hunted, from his home state of Alabama east, west, north, and south. And that was long before ATVs became as popular as they are today. I've also used ATVs to get to hunting spots for deer, big game, waterfowl, upland game, and small game across much of North America, and have discovered they're an invaluable tool.

ATVs can make many types of hunting more fun and more productive.

HAULING OUT DEER AND BIG GAME

Many years ago, Ben Lee showed me the easy way to extract a buck from deep in the Alabama swamps. He simply tied a rope around the antlers and pulled the animal out to the pickup. ATVs can indeed make getting your deer out of the woods easy, and dragging the carcass out is the simplest method. Tie a rope to the neck or back feet and take off. If the animal is a trophy and you intend to have the head mounted, however, this method isn't ideal. Dragging does strip hair off the hide, and you can damage the antlers if they catch on anything. Make sure the rope is attached to the bottom hitch, rather than tied to the top rack, to prevent the possibility of tipping the ATV over backward. Drive in low gear range and be careful going up slopes, or sidehilling on steep hills. In the latter case, a big carcass can roll down the hill, tip the ATV over, and even pull it down the hill.

Sometimes you can't even get an ATV to a downed animal, and in that case a good winch can be invaluable. I've used a Warn Kawasaki Winch on my Kawasaki Prairie 650 more than once, for removing animals from rugged spots deep in Ozark ravines.

A major help is hauling out deer and other game.

In some cases, you may be able to transport the deer on your ATV rack. It's extremely important, however, to make sure you don't overload the carrying capacity of your racks. Carrying a deer out on your ATV also requires some special attention to safety, especially on steep hills and in rough country. Four-wheelers can tip sideways or backward if they're loaded incorrectly, carrying too much weight, or driven carelessly. Also, make sure the deer is securely tied down. Lash the legs and head as close to the body as possible so they don't catch on trees and other obstacles. Go slow and in low gear range.

Getting the deer up onto the ATV rack can present another problem. I've tried to heft a 250-pound buck up onto my ATV, and it's a chore for one person. When you pick up one end, the other end limply slides away. A number of products are available for hoisting game up onto the vehicle, however. The original DeerLift hoist mounts directly on your machine and allows you to easily hoist the animal up and swing it into place. It's also available to fit pickup receiver hitches, allowing easy lifting of the deer up onto the pickup bed.

Pa-Paw's ATV Game Hoist has a horizontal boom attached to a telescopic, two-piece vertical shaft. The shaft fits to a bracket that can be attached to either ATV rack. It takes about 15 minutes to install the bracket, whether the cargo carrier has a basket-type rack or not. Attached to the lower portion of the vertical shaft is a manually operated winch. A rope from the winch passes through a pair of pulleys and terminates in a hook and pulley. The hoist boom can be extended up to 8 feet, and has a 300-pound capacity at 7 feet. A two-position support leg is fitted into the mounting socket to provide more support when hoisting bigger game. The leg adjusts to any ground-level condition. Not only can Pa-Paw's ATV Game Hoist lift the carcass up and onto the cargo rack, but it can also be used to hoist the animal up for dressing, or back at camp for hanging the carcass to allow it to drain and cool. The unit can be quickly and easily disassembled and stowed.

Of course, you can also use a trailer with your ATV to get game out of the woods, and if you're hauling more than one animal, a trailer might be your best choice. Although you can pick up a garden trailer at your local superstore, a better bet is an ATV trailer. These are more rugged, usually with off-road tires for more stability in off-road situations, yet are lightweight. The Swisher ATV Dump

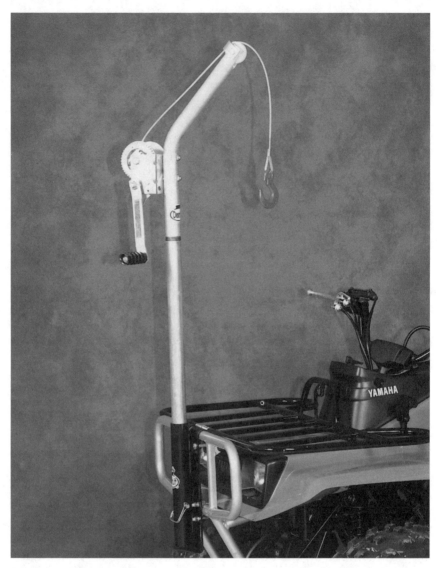

A number of game hoists are available to assist in getting deer and other game up on the ATV for transporting. (Photo courtesy Original DeerLift)

Cart from Bass Pro Shops is a good choice, as is the Cycle Country dump trailer from Hi-Per Sports. Kawasaki has a wagon with extended sides. The same safety rules apply when pulling a trailer, especially on steep hills.

A pull-behind trailer can be used to haul gear to the woods and game out. (Photo courtesy Otter Outdoors)

Utility vehicles with big cargo boxes make hauling deer even easier. The DeerLift hoist can be mounted onto the hitch receiver of the vehicle for easy lifting into the bed.

It's no trouble getting a deer out of the woods if you have an ATV and a few other tools.

HAULING GEAR

Hauling out game isn't the only use for your ATV. Both ATVs and utility vehicles are great for transporting stands to hunting areas. Utility vehicles with seating for more than one, plus cargo space, also make these chores easy. One tactic I've used is to mount a Hitch-Haul, such as that from Masterbuilt, on the 2-inch receiver hitch of a utility vehicle for toting out a deer. Don't do this on an ATV, however—you can greatly unbalance it.

SPEED SCOUTING

I have a number of permanent tree stands overlooking green fields and traditionally good breeding zone areas, areas that produce each year for deer hunting guests. I learned a long time ago, however, that versatility can make the real difference in whitetail hunting success. Deer patterns can shift, sometimes overnight, for a number of reasons. Over the past few years, I've discovered a tactic I call "speed scouting" on my Kawasaki ATV. Granted, this technique won't work in wilderness areas where deer rarely encounter motorized vehicles, but the deer in my part of the Ozarks hear ATVs and farm tractors all the time. Correctly done, speed scouting does less to disturb deer patterns than a hunter walking through the woods.

I scout the hunting areas beginning a month before the season opens, and can cover a lot of ground in a short amount of time. I'm primarily looking for scrapes, rubs, and evidence of feeding in fields. I also use the ATV for late-evening scouting, glassing feed fields from a distance. I am frequently off the vehicle at that time, seriously scouting and using the ATV to cover the distance between the hunting areas quickly and easily.

Once I determine that an area looks promising, I note it in a field notebook. Then I move tree stands to that area if necessary, cutting shooting lanes and generally doing all the fieldwork needed to ready the stand and area for the coming season. I strap an ordinary plastic

ATVs are great for hauling deer stands to the woods.

tub to the front rack and fill it with pruning shears, rope, flagging materials, and other tools and equipment needed for placing stands.

Then, once a week, I make a quick run to all the areas. This time I do the scouting from the seat of my ATV, and get in and out fast. I stay on the vehicle and use a pair of binoculars to examine scrapes, rubs, tracks, and trails from a distance. I don't disturb anything. I make my last scouting run a couple of days before the season opens, during midday to cause the least disturbance to the animals. I continue to monitor green fields and agricultural fields from a distance, again from the seat of my ATV, late in the evening. A good pair of lightweight binoculars is a must, and a good spotting scope gives me a good close-up look at beanfield bucks.

Tree stands that can be set up and moved instantly are the next part of the equation. Hang-on tree stands are extremely popular for this. I use ladder stands in most places, however. Even though they're bulky, they carry easily on an ATV, and set up quicker than hang-ons or even most climbers. I can have a stand set up, lock it down, and be out of there in about 10 minutes. I have an original Baker ladder stand that is definitely old enough to vote, and I wish someone would remake it. Aluminum with a wooden top that I've replaced twice, it features two sections that snap together, and the top lifts up and snaps down for an instant stand. It's extremely lightweight and easy to maneuver. I also have an old Warren and Sweat steel model that folds down completely in one piece and is easily transported on an ATV, although it is heavier than the Baker. One of my favorites is the API Grand Slam Lite Ladder Supreme. It weighs only 19 pounds, has cushions to provide extreme comfort, and sets up quickly. It even features a shooting rail.

If you're moving a number of tree stands, an ATV trailer such as one from Otter Outdoors is a good choice. For transporting or moving only one or two of them, the API ATV Carry-All fits onto the back of cargo racks and has multiple options for vertical or horizontal attachment. Cabela's has an excellent ATV Tree Stand Carrier that also can be used to carry hard-sided bow or gun cases. Bass Pro's Treestand Buddy and ATV Totem are great for transporting tree stands.

Speed scouting and moving stands don't have to be relegated to the preseason. Don't be afraid to move a stand that isn't producing, no matter what the date. Sometimes moving only 50 to 100 yards can make a real difference. Again, the ATV makes the move quick and easy. I once moved a stand at midday during the second week

Once stand locations are determined, stands can be quickly and easily hauled to the site and erected.

of the season, and the biggest buck of the year was taken from it five hours later, just as the sun was going down. One season I noted a change in the use of scrapes, and moved a stand 25 yards to provide a better bow shot. That stand also produced a nice buck.

ATVs for Waterfowlers

"I've found them," said my son Mark over the phone. "They're on the big flat up by Possum Creek, and there's got to be 1,000 mallards using the area. That's the good part. The bad news is that there's an old road that goes within 100 yards of the area, but it's pure mud. I walked in and somebody had already been stuck in there big time. Looks like they had to get a tractor to get out. We can't get a vehicle within 2 miles, and I don't think old Charlie can begin to walk that far. We'll have to use your ATV and trailer to get everything in."

A four-wheeler can get waterfowlers into some great places, and haul a lot of gear as well. I've used a Kawasaki Prairie 300 for hauling in materials to assemble blinds before the season and for hauling out

Waterfowlers will find ATVs invaluable for getting big bags of decoys as well as hunters to blinds.

the blinds afterward. I also hunt with several hundred decoys, and the ATV is great for hauling the big bags. I often pull a Poke Boat loaded with more decoys behind my boat. The kayaklike craft is extremely light but ultrasturdy, and it can be used not only to bring in decoys but also to set them out and even as a chase boat if a cripple gets out into open and deep water, too far for the retrievers.

A lot of gear, especially decoy bags, can simply be attached to existing ATV racks and tied down with rubber cords. Rack extensions, however, can increase the carrying capacity of your machine, and most manufacturers offer them. A metal basket that fits onto the back of the ATV, such as the Cabela's ATV Drop Basket Rack, can haul a lot more decoys. Weekend Warrior has a dandy back basket with a 3-inch-thick back support cushion. Tamarack Quad Trunks can easily carry a huge amount of gear in both front and rear boxes, and are easily installed or removed. Decoy bags can also be secured on top. Cycle Country has a huge rear-rack utility box that will hold tons of waterfowling gear.

An even better choice is a trailer that can be pulled behind the ATV. You can haul a lot more gear, plus hunters, in some trailers. Although some small utility trailers will work, most feature road tires that can be a problem in the muck of waterfowling country. The best trailers feature off-road or high-flotation tires.

Otter Outdoors offers three exceptionally strong and durable trailer models, featuring high-speed tapered roller bearings with wheel hubs that can be greased and 18-inch tires that can handle loads up to 1,500 pounds. A spring-loaded latch mechanism allows the heavy-duty polyethylene body to tilt for dumping. Cycle Country also has a utility trailer. The Swisher ATV Dump Cart, available from Bass Pro, has 13 cubic feet of cargo space, a tilting bed, and flotation-type tires. Weekend Warrior has a big four-wheel trailer that can double as a highway trailer.

GUN AND BOW RACKS

Transporting a gun or bow on an ATV can be a hassle at the least, and downright dangerous at the worst. You can simply tie a gun or bow in place, but it eventually gets snagged and always comes loose. Any number of racks and holders are available to make the chore easier and safer while providing protection for your gun or bow.

Guns are easier to transport, and many ATV manufacturers offer gun racks. Kawasaki, for example, offers a molded fiberglass Gun Boot, similar to that used for horse packing, that holds the gun securely, safely, and out of the weather. The hard case straps securely in place. Polaris has a Gun Scabbard, also a hard case, that straps to the rack. The company offers a dual pack rack that holds two guns, as well as a single model. A similar hard case that bolts directly to the front rack is available from Mad Dog Gear. The company also has open gun racks that bolt to the rear carrier, as well as one that bolts to the handlebars.

A number of bolt-on gun racks are available from All Rite Products, Inc. The Freedom Holder Double-Hook ATV Rack from Rugged Gear is an innovative design that can be mounted to any round or square bar, handlebars, and most racks—including composites. The unique ribbed swivel mechanism allows the rack to be mounted in nonparallel positions, while the hooks swivel and lock parallel. The rack can be used to hold guns, bows, or tools. API Outdoors, well known for quality tree stands, also carries a full line of ATV accessories including the Universal Front Gun Rack, a handlebar-mounted rack that carries two guns.

Guns must be transported safely on ATVs, which means they must be unloaded and stored in a protective case. (Photo courtesy Kawasaki)

Kolpin gun holders are available for utility vehicles as well.

Needless to say, all safety rules should be followed, and the guns must be unloaded while in transport.

Bows are a bit harder to transport, simply because they're larger, they're more cumbersome, and they tend to catch on everything along the trail, which often causes serious problems with alignment. Two styles are available for attaching to front ATV racks: vertical and horizontal. Both are available from Mad Dog Gear. Vertical models are available from All Rite Products, Inc., in single or double configurations in steel with rubber coating, or rubber-coated composite models. Mounting systems are available for either flat cargo carriers or those with rails. The API Easy Rider Bowholder mounts on the handlebars and is designed to prevent the possibility of getting your bow out of tune. Patented cushion clamps hold the bow firmly by the limbs, snugly balanced to the front of the handlebars. The best rack, however, is the API Power Pak ATV Bowholder. The Power Pak works on a unique system of tension-powered holding racks, and provides absolutely safe transport for any compound or recurve bow on the front ATV carrier. It even comes with a waterproof cover to protect your bow on rainy, sloppy days.

Bows are a bit more awkward to carry on ATVs, but a number of holders are available for guns, bows, and tools. (Photo courtesy All Rite Products)

If you're looking for a place for your "snake gun," CDS, Inc., sells a handy Pistol Holster and Pouch, perfect for carrying a sidearm on your ATV. It makes the gun easily accessible and is ambidextrous. The pouch on the opposite side is large enough to carry a full box of 3-inch shotgun shells; it attaches across the gas tank with adjustable straps.

A wide range of gun and bow racks are also available from both Bass Pro and Cabela's catalogs.

RACK IT, PACK IT, SACK IT: HOW TO CARRY MORE ON YOUR ATV

In addition to toting you to your hunting site, ATVs are often used to transport gear. One of the fastest-growing segments of the ATV market is the number of soft bags, hard cases, and aftermarket racks that can be added to increase the versatility of your vehicle.

Soft Bags

Many ATV manufacturers offer their own version of accessory bags and racks. These items are often sized or designed to fit specific

Utility vehicles make great "dog-wagons" as well as people carriers for shooting preserves and gun clubs. (Photo courtesy E-Z-GO)

ATVS can provide a means to getting to off-road fishing holes.

ATVs can also provide a way of carrying camping gear into the backcountry.

ATV models. For instance, Kawasaki has rack bags for their Prairie models. These include front and rear bags that are both 7 inches in height, have sturdy side stiffeners, and feature an egg-crate form inside the lid. A Prairie model seat bag is available to fit in front of the rear rack bag and on the back of the seat, adding even more storage. A tank bag is also available to fit over the tank in front of the driver. Additional space can be had with fender bags that fit in front of each fender.

Several years ago I went on an ATV adventure, testing the Yamaha Kodiak on Kodiak Island, Alaska. It was a black-tailed deer hunt with extended trips on the island. My test ATV had a front bag with a clear plastic map pocket on the top. This bag made it extremely easy to follow the unmarked trails on our ride. A similar bag is available from Cabela's, also weatherproof. In addition, Cabela's carries Pro Series Saddle Bags that fit over the tank, as well as fender bags and a big utility rear rack bag that is contoured to fit over rear ATV racks. This bag features three separate zippered compartments and a padded additional seat for resting on the trail. Kawasaki's Tank Bag also has a clear map case.

A wide variety of soft packs and bags can be used to help ease the hauling of gear. (Photo courtesy Suzuki)

Bass Pro carries the Mad Dog Gear Rack Bag, a huge cargo bag measuring 18 x 12 x 36 inches, with all sides padded for extra protection; a zipper extends around three of them. The bag has eight D-rings to secure extra gear on top, with hook-and-loop closures to hold a gun or extra gear. Also from Bass Pro is the Mad Dog Gear Cooler Rack Bag, a soft-sided, insulated waterproof cooler that holds up to 48 quarts. The Pro ATV bags from Bass Pro include two rear rack bags, one of them oversized with five compartments; two water bottle holders; and two removable compartments with belt loops.

Also from Bass Pro are a number of Kolpin bags, including front/rear rack bags, and the new Kolpin Sealtector ATV Rainproof Luggage Bag, which has all seams electronically sealed. Its walls are made of rigid, closed-cell foam with a fully lined interior and aluminum reinforcing material.

Hard Cases

ATV hard cases provide the ultimate in weather protection, and also protect delicate items such as cameras and binoculars. The ultimate

Hard racks can also be utilized for toting bulkier items. (Photo courtesy Kolpin)

in rear rack storage may be Cabela's ATV Storage Box, constructed of weatherproof polyethylene with weatherproof stripping along the inside edges. Also available from Cycle Country, the box features a padded seat and backrest for resting during trail stops. A front storage box with a fairing or windshield is available from Cabela's. The windshield protects you from wind and snagging branches. The Cabela's ATV Dry Box fits on the rear rack, but also has a rear-mounting bracket that allows the box to sit behind instead of on the rack, adding even more storage to the ATV.

Bass Pro carries Kolpin Contoured Cargo Boxes for both front and rear ATV racks. These boxes feature a weathertight gasket to keep out the elements. The Mad Dog Gear rear cargo box, available from Bass Pro, includes a rubber seal with a metal liner for watertight protection. From Plano is the Rear-Mount ATV Box with double wall construction and a removable lid that opens from the front or back. A smaller, front-mounted box has a protective foam insert and a large lift-out tray. I frequently use it on my Prairie 650 to tote cameras. If you're looking for sturdy, the Bass Pro Black Tread ATV boxes are all metal. Two sizes mount on either front or rear racks.

Aluma Sport has both a large and a small aluminum, powder-coated box. The boxes are also available in Mossy Oak Break-Up camouflage. CDS carries both a Magnum Cajun Dri-Stor Dry Box and a smaller version. The magnum version is lockable. Both will fit on most front or rear ATV racks. The company offers rear-mounted brackets, too, that site the units off the back of the rear rack.

Racks

Most ATV manufacturers sell a variety of rack extensions. These extensions usually add height to the normally flat rack, allowing you to fasten more and bulkier items to the vehicle. Full metal racks, or more appropriately "baskets," are also available. Cabela's ATV Basket and Flat Racks are made of 14-gauge expanded metal, are available for both front and rear, and are 6.25 inches high. Their Drop Basket Rack fits on the rear rack; the back portion extends out past the rear ATV rack and drops down below it, adding more storage space for bulky items such as coolers, fuel cans, and tools. Another Cabela's exclusive is the ATV Hitch-Haul, which fits

Arctic Cat Speed Rack Platform has racks with receivers to hold a wide variety of accessories. (Photo courtesy Arctic Cat)

into the hitch receiver of ATVs and provides carrying space for coolers and other large items. The CDS Utility Rack pad provides a nonskid surface and can be custom-fit to any rack with a utility knife.

Bass Pro has a large Mad Dog Gear Back Basket made of rugged high-density polyethylene, as well as Strongbuilt expanded metal baskets for both front and rear. Their Universal Drop Basket Rack fits on the rear rack and adds storage space for large items. Tack on the Bass Pro Haul It All for the receiver hitch and you can carry lots of gear, including tents and coolers. The ATV Totem and Treestand Buddy from Bass Pro makes it easy to transport tree stands to the site. Their ATV Chain Saw Mount and Wing Pro Tool Mount are designed to tote tools to the woods as well. CDS Chain Saw Mount easily and safely totes chain saws, while their Utility Tool rack can be used to carry shovels, rakes, and gear for such chores as prescribed burns for wildlife management.

Most of us have resorted to a messy combination of bungee chords, tiedown straps, and even milk crates to attach any number of items and gear to ATVs when heading to our hunting spots. Arctic

Arctic Cat MRP Rapid Blind fits the Speed Rack platform to provide an instant hunting blind, or ice shanty right on your ATV.

Cat has just introduced an alternative to the strap-and-pray method they call the MultiRack Platform, or MRP. Using an open-channel, receiver-type design on the front and rear racks, hunters can affix many of the 20-plus accessory attachments to the MRP in a matter of seconds. The "slide-in" accessory attachments, many of which are designed for waterfowl and big-game hunting, are held securely in place with a simple pin. The result: maximized use of the 100- to 200-pound load capacity of the front/rear racks, secured gear, and a new level of usability.

For the waterfowler, a weatherproof cargo box provides easily accessed dry storage. Rack extensions with tall sides make it possible to haul two dozen decoys, and a cooler attachment doubles as a carryall for shell containers. These are in addition to the gun rack/utility bar and a host of other box- and basket-type attachments. Big-game hunters can opt for a similar supply of useful attachments, including gun scabbard, tool/gear lock (perfect for tree stands), water jug holder, expansion table, and more. These can be quickly removed for an after-the-hunt trail ride. The MultiRack Platform comes on the Arctic Cat 400 4x4 Automatic MRP and 500 4x4 Automatic MRP ATVs. MRP attachments are also available for fishing, farming, camping, and construction.

Regardless of what you wish to pack, sack, or rack, there's a product to fit your machine.

Concealing Your ATV

Once you get all the gear and hunters to the blind or stand, the next step is to camouflage your four-wheeler. Many manufacturers now offer camouflage models; camo tape can also be used. Camoclad ATV Camouflage Kits, available from Bass Pro, have long-lasting, self-adhesive vinyl that can be cut to any size or shape to provide the ultimate system for converting a shiny showroom ATV into a hunting machine. Walk-Winn and Avery Outdoors offer excellent, lightweight camouflage ATV covers that can be quickly thrown over your unit to hide it.

Arctic Cat's MRP Rapid Blind

Arctic Cat's MRP Series ATVs are more rabbit than turtle, but they do share something with the tortoise. These unique ATVs allow you to take your "home"—or rather hunting blind—with you. Hunting from a ground blind is extremely effective for turkeys and deer, not to mention waterfowl. Unfortunately, quite often toting in a blind, or gathering materials and constructing one, takes time and effort. And you're pretty well committed to the blind and the location.

The new Rapid Blind from Arctic Cat is a quality clamshell-type blind that can be easily mounted on the vehicle's front and rear racks within seconds, and without tools. The blind is firmly held in place while traveling to the blind location. Once you reach your destination, simply pull the internal-frame Rapid Blind over you and your Arctic Cat ATV. Within minutes, you're fully enclosed in a comfortable blind that offers weather protection and concealment. At 89 inches high, 88 inches wide, and 100 inches in length, the Rapid Blind has plenty of elbow room for at least two people. Multiple zip-out windows provide viewing and shooting opportunities in all directions, whether you're targeting deer, elk, turkeys, or ducks and geese. Access is easy through a front door. Additional camouflage roof netting allows waterfowlers to watch skyward in all directions, yet without spooking birds. A quick-release system pulls the netting back instantly for shooting. The blind cover is constructed of heavy-duty Cordura fabric, available in either Mossy Oak Shadow Grass (Waterfowl Rapid Blind package) or Mossy Oak New Break-Up (Big Game Rapid Blind package) camouflage patterns. Camo tabs on all sides allow you to fasten natural vegetation, such as rushes or grass, for further concealment.

Ice fishermen will also appreciate the Icefish Rapid Shack package, which comes in a highly visible blue. The Rapid Blind is available on 11 Arctic Cat ATVs, from their 300 4x4 MRP up to their 650 4x4 Auto MRP.

With the other Arctic Cat MRP System accessory racks on the ATV, you can even tote in folding chairs, a cooler, decoys, and all the hunting gear you'll need for a day of comfort. The system is engineered with innovative open channels on both the front and rear racks of MRP models. The open channels are designed to accept numerous slide-on accessory racks, baskets, or attachments, including gun carrying cases. The accessories secure in seconds with locking pins for rattle-free operation. Nine MRP packages, designed for specific applications, are available, including construction, ranching, fishing, camping, lawn care/landscape, Remington big game, and Rapid Blind packages. More than 40 slide-on accessory racks/attachments can be had; you can mix and match, choosing the various attachments desired.

With the Arctic Cat Rapid Blind and MRP accessory packages, not only is it easy to haul your gear and set up, but if you don't like your location, you can almost instantly take down the blind, pick up your decoys or other gear, and move to another spot.

UPLAND GAME HUNTING

Utility vehicles can make upland game hunting easy, especially for older hunters or those unable to make long walks. ATVs are also great for shooting preserves or areas with a lot of land to hunt. Hunters can simply follow the dogs with the utility vehicle. A number of dog boxes are available to fit the cargo areas. Custom-built models feature more seating, plus dog boxes so you can haul more than one extra hunter. The Pack Mule ATV trailer from Brewer Implement Company holds two adults plus gear, and models are available with dog boxes. Essex has a unit specially designed for bird hunting that can replace the bed of the Kawasaki Mule. Their Ultimate Bird Hunting Rig features a dog box with seating for four.

HUNTING RULES AND REGULATIONS

It's illegal to hunt off an ATV in most states. And it's unethical. The exception is a disabled person, for whom an ATV sometimes provides the only means to hunt. Follow all rules and regulations concerning the use of motorized vehicles during hunting season. Make sure you wear plenty of safety orange, and have some tied to your vehicle, during rifle deer and big-game season.

FISHING

Bank-bound anglers can also appreciate an ATV's ability to get to those hard-to-reach fishing holes. We used ATVs on Alaska's Kodiak Island to get to several excellent salmon streams. ATVs can make it easy to reach those backcountry hot spots. Utility vehicles can also be used to haul a friend as well as comfortable chairs and coolers with lunch and beverages.

CAMPING

ATV camping is a lot of fun—more so than car camping or back-packing, in some instances. Anything you can haul on your back and more can be carried on your ATV. An ATV, however, can get you farther back in the boonies than you might wish if you have a breakdown or trouble. Experts suggest carrying extra gas, water, spare tire or plugs, and a tire pump. Always let someone know where you're going and when you expect to return. Going with a buddy or friend makes the trip even more enjoyable, and someone can go for help if problems arise.

CHAPTER

6

Food Plots and Planting

Food plots offer great advantages in providing nutrition for deer, turkeys, and other wild game. Of course, they can also draw and hold wild game to your property. Food plots are actually nothing more than big gardens. In most cases, simply throwing seed on the ground won't work. For a food plot to be productive, the ground must be properly tilled and fertilized, the seed spread, and then covered or rolled into place. Otherwise you're just wasting time and money.

ATVs, or UTVs and a number of accessories can make planting food plots for wildlife easy, even in hard-to-reach spots.

139

If you have heavy-duty gardening or farm equipment and the food plots are easily accessible, you can usually work them up and plant them with that equipment. Sometimes, however, food-plot areas are not readily accessible, and many people simply don't have the larger farming or gardening equipment necessary for working several acres of soil. You may, however, already have the key ingredient for easy food-plot planting—the ATV you use in your deer or turkey camp for getting to hunting areas, hauling deer stands, and other chores. I plant more than a dozen food plots each year on our property, which is managed primarily for white-tailed deer and turkeys. I've found the chore simple with an ATV and accessories.

Planting food plots with an ATV does require some special tools, and more and more accessories are becoming available. Some ATV manufacturers sell their own tillage and other accessories. Check with your local dealer or contact the company for a listing of what's available. You can also buy tilling and planting equipment by mail order.

Tillage equipment runs from light to heavy duty. You will need a fairly large ATV to use with the heavier pieces, and those with a three-point hitch. A four-wheel-drive ATV model can also be helpful in heavier soils. Most utility vehicles are fitted with a rear hitch or have a hitch as an option, and can also be used for this chore.

I've tested ATVs and utility vehicles on numerous tillage tools, including a 4WD Kawasaki Prairie 300, a medium-sized machine, with good results. The harder groundbreaking chores are easier with larger machines, such as the 650 and 700cc models. Here are some methods for creating and planting food plots, along with suggestions for equipment to make the job easier.

CLEARING

Clearing brush and timber, overgrown clear-cuts, or old pastures for food plots requires a lot of hard work if you don't have a bulldozer. On the other hand, it's cheaper if you do the work yourself—and you don't damage the soil as much as with a dozer. A small chain saw and a brushcutter or brushcutter attachment for a heavy-duty weed cutter will do the job quite nicely on brush and small saplings. An ATV trailer can be used for hauling equipment to the site for easy clearing. If you intend to do double duty and use the cleared saplings and such for firewood, you can haul out the wood on the trailer.

To clear larger trees, Bombardier carries a full line of NovaJack timbering products for ATVs. These allow low-impact logging, and include a logging trailer and a logging arch. The trailer features four tires, log cradles, and a winch. The logging arch has a set of single wheels and a unique system that lifts the front end of the log for easy skidding. You will need a larger-model ATV, such as the Bombardier Traxter XT, to use these tools.

Once the trees, brush, and saplings have been cut, however, they will quickly resprout, resulting in an area completely covered with sprouts within one summer growth period. To kill the sprouts, to prevent them from regrowing after cutting, or to kill sprouts and unwanted brush without mechanical clearing, you can use an herbicide, such as BASF's Arsenal or Plateau, in a sprayer that mounts on the back rack of your ATV, or on a trailer you can pull with your ATV or utility vehicle.

If old fields and overgrown clearings need to be thinned of trees, ATV trailers can be used to haul away the wood to be used for firewood.

A tank sprayer is a very important tool for spraying herbicides to kill back vegetation before planting, or to control weeds in the food plot. Tank sprayers are also available as either ATV rack-mounted or pull types. ATV rack-mounted models are the most common and hold from 16 to 25 gallons. They may be spot sprayers for spraying individual plants, or boom sprayers for spraying wide swaths. The best of the boom sprayers have breakaway booms that snap back if an object is struck, and can also be switched from spot to boom.

Cycle Country offers a wide variety of ATV sprayers. Their AG Commercial ATV Sprayer features a 25-gallon tank with the sump powered by a SHURFLO Pump (3.0 GPM at 45 psi). Standard equipment includes a pressure relief valve with return agitation, a liquid-filled pressure gauge, an in-line clear bowl strainer, and an 18-inch poly hand gun. It can also be outfitted with either a 10- or 16-foot spring-loaded breakaway, fold-behind boom. The booms offer diaphragm check-valve nozzle bodies with quick caps and 50 mesh screens and tips. These prevent costly drips and leaks between fields. Also available are rack-mounted ATV spot sprayers and a 30- and 55-gallon trailer sprayer. A large variety of ATV rack and pull-behind sprayers are available from Cabela's, Bass Pro, Kawasaki, Weekend Warrior, Hi-Per Sports, Arctic Cat, Northern Tool, and Polaris.

If you need to haul logs, a number of ATV lumbering products are available from NovaJack. (Photo courtesy Bombardier)

Herbicides are often used to keep hardwoods from resprouting in fields and clearings. ATV sprayers such as the unit shown from Cycle Country make the chore quick and easy.

SOIL PREPARATION

Just as with a good garden, proper soil preparation is necessary for a food plot. ATV equipment for soil preparation consists of three types: single-hitch lightweight, single-hitch heavyweight, and three-point hitch. The first two utilize the existing hitch on your ATV. The lighter-weight implements can be pulled by some of the smaller ATVs, and of course all the larger models.

ATV TOOLS

Groundbreaking implements are available separately or in some unique (one-piece) tools that can do more than one chore, or even do two or more chores at a time. I've had the opportunity to test just about all the ATV accessory tools on the market, and there are similarities as well as differences. These tools are not cheap, and it's important to choose the proper ones to suit your situation.

Groundbreaking and soil preparation are the hardest and most time-consuming chores. If you're breaking new ground in some soils, you may need fairly heavy equipment, and some tools are light in weight. Rocky soil is another common problem in many food-plot locations. The lighter-weight tools may take quite a bit more time and several passes. Some landowners prefer to have the groundbreaking done by a neighbor with larger farming equipment; then they can fertilize and plant the seed. This requires only an ATV-mounted spreader.

In some instances, however, food plots may be hard for larger equipment to get to, or you may not have a neighbor or close-at-hand person with groundbreaking equipment. Or you may simply prefer to do the chores yourself. In any event, you'll need groundbreaking tools. The Mossy Oak BioLogic by Tufline Sportsman line includes two discs, 52- and 64-inch cutting-width models. All feature 7.5-inch blades, adjustable gang cutting angles, flange-mounted sealed ball bearings, and a ratchet lift transport gauge wheel system or an electric hydraulic lift system as an option. These are heavy tools and are recommended only for liquid-cooled transmission ATVs. The discs are available in two series. The Series 2 models are rated for 300 and 400cc ATVs and feature a 2-inch frame. Series 1 models are rated for 450cc and large four-wheel drive ATVs and have a heavy-duty 3-inch tube framework. One of the most intriguing ground-working tools I've seen is the GroundHog from Tufline. This is a small, easily attached, but very aggressive groundbreaking machine that uses the weight of the ATV and can even be used with smaller machines.

A number of groundbreaking tools are available. Some, such as the Tufline Mossy Oak BioLogic heavy-duty offset disk, require a fairly powerful, liquid-cooled ATV or UTV.

The Tufline GroundHog is a unique, small disk that uses the weight of the machine for quick and deep cutting action.

Lighter weight tools, such as the Weekend Warrior Tandem offset disk can be used successfully with smaller ATVs.

The Weekend Warrior Tandem Disc is offset style and has a 64-inch cutting width. It features notched blades, pneumatic tires that serve as a depth gauge, and an electric actuator for raising and lowering. The company also has a 60-inch cultivator with spring shanks that can be used for cultivating prepared soils.

One of the most important steps in creating food plots with tiny seed such as clover is culti-packing or smoothing the soil and packing the seed down into the soil, but not burying it. The Tufline ATV BCP Culti-Packer, featuring cast-iron packer wheels, not only does a great job of smoothing the seed bed, but also packs the seed in place. The wheels are mounted on a heavy-duty gang assembly with 3-inch-square tube steel and a 48-inch working width.

The Tartar Gate Company, in partnership with Hunter's Specialties, also has a line of Hunter's Specialties Terrain Tough ATV implements and accessories, including disc harrows, culti-packer and disc/culti-packer combos, seeders, sprayers, and other accessories.

Abby Manufacturing Company has a 300 pound ground-driven, pull-behind spreader that spreads up to 30 feet. The AMC spreader has corrosion resistant stainless steel and polyethylene construction. (Photo courtesy AMC)

Three-point hitch ground-breaking tools are also available. These utilize the weight of the machine and driver to create down pressure. With the hitch attached, various tools can quickly and easily be changed such as with this Cycle Country hitch and tools. (Third photo courtesy Cycle Country)

Arctic Cat Speed Point is a unique and easy-to-use 3-point hitch system. You can change from moldboard plow to tandem disc to cultivator in less than a minute.

Three-point hitch groundbreaking tools are available from Cycle Country, Polaris, and Arctic Cat. They utilize a bracket attached to the rear of the machine. A variety of implements can be attached to the bracket. The weight of the machine creates down pressure, with quicker and more even cutting and smoothing of the soil. The unique Arctic Cat Speed Point system uses an easy-access three-point attachment on the ATV so you can change from a moldboard plow to tandem disc to a cultivator in less than a minute.

Polaris also has a 3-point hitch system that fits their ATVs as well as their Ranger UTVs. (Photo courtesy Polaris)

Using multiple tools means you first break the ground with a disc, then spread fertilizer and seed, and then follow with a disc to bury large seed, or a culti-packer for smaller seeds. This requires several pieces of equipment for you to purchase, store, and transport. Multiple-use tools can cut down on storage area, as well as the time spent moving the tools back and forth to the food plot.

The Plotmaster from Tecomate was the first tool that combined several tools in one. I've tested each model of the Plotmaster as it has become available. The Plotmaster 400 is a 4-foot heavy-duty, tractor-grade tool that is scaled down and designed for ATVs. You will need at least a 400cc four-wheel-drive ATV for most soils. The Plotmaster starts with an all-steel implement featuring 16-inch discs that can turn even the hardest soils into soft seed beds. The discs can be angled to create lesser or more aggressive cutting. Following the disc is a spring-steel plow system that can be set to cut even deeper, or to create planting furrows for a variety of seeds. The entire unit is raised and lowered by an electrical hydraulic actuator with the control box mounted on your ATV. The Plotmaster also features an electric seeder that can be set to seed anything from tiny clover seeds to corn. Finally, following the seeder is a culti-packer system that rolls the soil flat and packs the earth for good seed–soil contact.

Multiuse tools, such as the Plotmaster, have all the tools in one. This saves on storage, time, and problems in transporting and hooking up multiple tools.

Plotmaster can do separate chores or do it all at one time. It can break ground, plant seed, and cover seed.

An optional system also features a bar drag and an attachable chain drag that preps the soil into baseball-infield smoothness, necessary for clover or alfalfa. The chores can be done one at a time; if the soil is fairly well worked, though, you can disc, plow and furrow, drop seed, cover, and culti-pack all in one pass.

A number of optional accessories make the Plotmaster even more versatile. This includes a moldboard plow and a grain drill

A variety of accessories makes the Plotmaster even more versatile.

attachment that plants seeds such as soybeans in even rows. Other attachments include a spreader, de-thatching rake, one-row planter, 15- or 25-gallon sprayer, rolling basket, and scraper blade.

ATV rack-mounted spreaders are available from Cycle Country, EarthWay products from Northern Tool, and also some ATV manufacturers, including Arctic Cat. One of the problems with many rack-mounted spreaders is that their mounting brackets are not standard to fit all ATVs. Most of these mount hanging out behind the ATV rack and have 100 pounds or less capacity. One model is available that holds 250 pounds, but should only be used on larger utility vehicles, not ATVs.

These units all run off a 12-volt motor that attaches to your ATV electrical system. A pull-type spreader will tote more weight in the form of fertilizer than you can safely haul on an ATV rack, but may be somewhat harder to transport back into some of those out-of-the-way spots. Tufline's BioLogic series of spreaders are available with 300- or 600-pound capacities. They are ground-gear driven, which means the wheels drive the spreader as they turn; you don't have to hassle with an electric wire to your ATV, and they are available with 20 x 4.5-inch high-clearance tires. Adams Fertilizer Equipment has a 750-pound-capacity seeder that is constructed entirely of stainless steel and is also ground driven.

The Tufline pull-type spreader is safer and easier to use than an ATV-mounted model. Three hundred and 400 pound capacity models are available.

The Swisher Quadivator also comes with a wide array of implements combined in one pull-type tool. (Photo courtesy Polaris)

The last implement needed is a heavy-duty mower. Swisher offers several heavy-duty ATV-pulled models. Their Trail Cutter mowers are designed for the tough stuff and will cut most tree stems up to 1.5 inches in diameter. They feature a 44-inch cutting deck and a 10.5-horsepower Briggs and Stratton engine. An offset hitch allows mowing off to the side.

The Weekend Warrior Brush Cut Mower features a 12- or 13-horsepower engine choice and 48-inch-wide cut that will rip through tall weeds, overgrown brush, and even small trees. The Brush Cut mower also features an offset hitch.

Swisher, long known for high-quality lawn mowers, also has a great multipurpose unit, the Quadivator, that works with a garden tractor or ATV. The Quadivator comes complete with electric depth control, which can be mounted on your ATV or garden tractor. It can be converted to a rake, tiller, irrigator, lawn roller, chemical applicator, aerator, disc, or plow. The tandem disc installs with a single bolt. An optional dump box attaches to the frame, and the auto open–close tailgate allows easy dumping from the operator's seat. There's even a box scraper/leveler that is ideal for landscaping and other leveling chores. Other optional equipment includes hilling moldboards, a potato/vegetable digger, a lawn irrigation plow, a barbed-wire dispenser, lawn roller, and a lawn chemical applicator. The Quadivator is also available from Polaris dealers.

A broadcast seeder, such as this unit from Moultrie, can be used to broadcast seed and/or fertilizer.

Polaris offers several mowers in front-mounted and pull-behind styles, including the 44-inch pull-behind brush mower. It's ideal for use in overgrown areas and topping off food plots. It has a powerful 10.5-horsepower Tecumseh engine and cuts brush up to 1.5 inches in diameter. The Polaris brush mower features breakaway blades and a "Stump Jumper" spindle protector. Polaris also offers three models of finishing mowers with decks ranging from 45 to 60 inches.

Not only can these accessories make preparing food plots easy, but they can also do double duty around your lawn and garden, mowing, breaking ground, and planting.

Food plots require summer mowing to keep weeds down. Pull-type, ATV mowers are available for working food plots and keeping trails cleared.

Recreational Opportunities and Responsibilities

A 1999 survey found that the number of Americans participating in outdoor recreation has steadily increased since 1994, and that ATVing has become an important part of the outdoor recreational scene. This includes hunters, anglers, landowners, and a large group of people who simply use ATVs for pleasure riding, sightseeing, and wildlife-watching. Researchers say that more and more families are answering the call of the great outdoors. My family enjoys the use of these vehicles on our property. A leisurely trail ride, sometimes on ATVs, sometimes with my family and grandkids in a utility vehicle, usually results in seeing lots of wildlife, including deer, turkeys, geese, ducks, quail, rabbits, and songbirds. We've discovered that if you ride on by, most wildlife tends to either ignore you or slip quietly away—usually just out of sight. Used properly, ATVs do not spook wildlife, but offer lots of viewing pleasure.

TRAIL RIDING FUN

Trail riding is one of the purest forms of ATV fun. It can be done individually or in groups, on private or public lands, and sometimes on lands set aside for ATV trail use. The Paiute ATV Trail System in Utah is one example of an area specifically set aside for ATV use. In fact, it was the first all-inclusive and multiuse ATV trail system in the United States. It has major trailheads, ATV access at local towns, and more than 800 miles of marked trails, with many side trails, loops, and spurs specifically designated for ATV use. In addition, 1,000 miles of linked forest roads are also available for ATV operation in the area.

ATV trail riding individually or in a group is a very popular outdoor recreation.

The Paiute ATV Trail System also allows you to connect with other major state trail systems, including the Great Western Trail and the Dixie and Manti–La Sal National Forests. Those interested should buy the guidebook *The Paiute ATV Trail System*, by Darlene Uzelac, Robert Uzelac, and Roger Foisy. It is available from Silver Sage Enterprises, PO Box 555, American Fork, UT 84003, or from various retail outlets in the Paiute Trail area. Paiute Trail information is available online at www.atvutah.com. One of the unique features of this trail system is that connecting towns allow street riding of ATVs. Riders can follow the trail into town for breakfast, lunch, or other recreation, then simply hit the trail for another small burg. Each September the town of Richfield, Utah, hosts the Rocky Mountain ATV Jamboree with coordinated trail rides and a host of organized events.

If you're interested in discovering more ATV trails, contact the National Off-Highway Vehicle Conservation Council (NOHVCC) by calling 800-348-6487 or visiting www.nohvcc.org. The organization is dedicated to educating and helping riders find a place to ride. You also may wish to contact the individual organizations in your state. Most are affiliated with the council; you can find them by calling the above number or visiting the Web site.

A number of ATV trail systems, such as the Paiute ATV Trail, offer lots of opportunities for off-road ATVing.

Local ATV clubs can often provide opportunities for organized trail rides.

If you're new to ATVs and wish to try your hand locally, the first step is to talk to your dealer about riding possibilities in your area. ATV clubs are also a great way of finding riding areas and events, as well as making new friends. Most are also associated with the NO-HVCC, and many local area clubs are also listed at www.nohvcc.org. Many local clubs have their own Web sites, on which they post meetings and coming events. These links are available through the NOHVCC Web site.

Additional information on trails is available from www.recreation.gov.

PREPARING FOR THE TRIP

The first step is to determine the trail you wish to ride. Obtain maps of the trail or area and make sure the trail is open to off-road use. Acquire regulations and rules regarding the use of the trail—such as width of vehicles, age limitations, training prerequisites, and the necessary registration. Some states require a permit for out-of-state participants. Make a plan of your route of travel. Let someone know your route, leave a copy of your marked map with them, and let them know when you expect to return.

ATV Checkup

Check your ATV to make sure it's mechanically ready for the trail. You should, for example, make sure that the headlights work, that the suspension doesn't have loose or worn joints, and that the shocks are in good shape. Visually inspect the handlebars to make sure they are straight, that there is no looseness in the steering, and that the grips are securely in place. Check the condition of the tires, and make sure they are inflated to the correct pressure. The wheels should turn freely without binding, but not have excessive play. Check all wheel bolts and make sure there are no cracks or dents in the wheels.

Check brake pads, shoes, rotors, and drums, and replace if necessary. Make sure all control cables operate smoothly. Lubricate as needed. Lubricate all fittings, and check the oil level in the final gear drive at the rear axle.

Clean the air filter and make sure it is properly oiled. Check and change the engine/transmission oil as needed. If your vehicle has a

Before you ride, make a walk-around inspection. Check all steering and controls.

two-stroke engine, make sure the jetting is adjusted for the altitude you will be riding. Make sure the exhaust pipe, muffler, and spark arrestors are working.

Check the coolant level on liquid-cooled models. Clean dirt off the fins on the cylinder and cylinder head of air-cooled models.

EMERGENCY GEAR

You should carry a few tools and an emergency kit. The tools and supplies should include wrenches to fit; a spark plug wrench; a multifunction pocketknife with various screwdriver tips or screwdrivers; small vise grips; a hand tire pump; a tire plug repair kit; a replacement spark plug; hose clamps; a headlight bulb; duct tape; and nuts, bolts, or other fittings and fasteners appropriate for your ATV. All this should fit into a small toolbox that can be strapped to your vehicle.

An emergency kit should contain a quality flashlight with spare batteries, toilet paper, first-aid kit, water purification tablets, map, compass and signal mirror, tow strap, rope, pencil and paper,

Carry emergency gear including extra gas, water, tire repair kit, first-aid kit, and survival equipment.

waterproof matches and fire starter, space blanket, high-energy food, and, if possible, a portable CB radio or cellular phone. In addition, you should carry spare gasoline and drinking water (32 ounces per person). A folding or cable saw can be invaluable for clearing fallen trees from the trail.

Be prepared for weather changes. Get the latest weather forecast. ATV riding can be strenuous and at the same time can expose you to the elements. Wear and/or carry the appropriate clothing, including rain gear.

ON THE TRAIL

Obey trail signs, especially those regarding gate closures. Trails are usually closed for a reason—quite often to allow them to rejuvenate after heavy use, or perhaps because the area is too dangerous for safe riding. This also means you should stay out of designated wilderness areas or those areas marked with no vehicular traffic signs. Do not chase or hassle wildlife, and keep well away from animals rearing young.

Use common sense and courtesy on the trail. Stay on marked trails.

One of the most important rules is to be courteous to others on the trail, including other ATVers. If you meet mountain bikers, hikers, or horseback riders, pull off to the side; in the case of horseback riders, shut off your ATV so you don't spook the horses and cause an accident. Don't make sudden movements; do speak quietly. If you meet other ATVers on the trail, yield to those traveling uphill or passing.

When passing other ATVers or hikers, avoid the temptation to apply the throttle once you're past them. The noise and dust can create problems.

Stay on the marked trails and don't cut across switchbacks or blaze your own trail. Ride in the center of the trail to avoid widening it and creating trail rebuilding problems. Especially avoid areas off the trail that can be damaged by ATV use, including streambanks and lakeshores, steep hillsides, meadows, and marshes. Keep off soft, wet, and muddy roads that can be easily damaged by ATVs. Don't run over young trees, saplings, and brush.

In a group, maintain a safe distance between vehicles. Don't tailgate—it can cause accidents. If your ATV has a headlight, turn it on. If you're stopping unexpectedly for a reason, pull to the side of the trail and hold your arm and hand up.

Each rider in the group should have a map of the area, and it should be marked with predetermined rest stops and meeting places in case someone gets lost or has problems.

ATVs FOR KIDS

Many families use outdoor recreation as a way to form bonds and transfer important values to children. This is nothing new to hunting parents and grandparents, who have spent time together in the outdoors for generations. In recent years, ATVs have taken the hunting world by storm and have become an important facet of the sport. In fact, the hunting segment of the market has overtaken the general sports segment for many manufacturers. There's a great deal of interest in ATVs as hunting tools. Overall sporting goods sales rose 2 percent in 1999, while the ATV industry sales grew 31 percent in the same period.

With competition from other forms of recreation, including television, computer games, and the Internet, anything we as parents

Kids can also enjoy the fun of ATVs with the proper instructions and supervision. (Photo courtesy Suzuki)

and grandparents can do to increase kids' interest in the outdoors helps. Kids just naturally love the excitement and fun of riding ATVs, so one way to get them more involved is to properly introduce them to ATVs.

Like any motorized vehicles, ATVs are not toys. They can be dangerous if used improperly, or used by youngsters without supervision. With proper education, equipment, and supervision, however, ATVs can be a great tie to the outdoors. If you're thinking of introducing a youngster to ATVs, you must understand and abide by all safety precautions. Several important steps must be followed. You must first determine if the child is ATV ready in physical size, strength, coordination, and maturity. Then the proper ATV must be

A number of youth model ATVs are available, even some for kids age six to eleven, including the Polaris Scrambler 50. (Photo courtesy Polaris)

matched to the child. Following is a table that matches rider size with recommended engine size, prepared by the Specialty Vehicle Institute of America.

ATV Size	Minimum Age
Over 90cc	16 years
70cc–90cc	12 years
Under 70cc	6 years

Parents or guardians should not permit youngsters to ride an ATV that is not recommended for their age group. And while a youth may be of the recommended age to ride a particular size of ATV, not all youngsters have the strength, size, skills, or judgment to operate one safely.

Protective gear and clothing must be provided for the child, and this includes an approved helmet, gloves, long-sleeved shirt/jacket, over-the-ankle boots, goggles/face shield, and long pants. Gear must fit properly. For instance, the helmet must be snug but not tight, and it must be properly fastened.

The next step is to educate yourself about ATV safety and proper riding techniques. This allows you to teach safe and proper riding methods to your youngster. One excellent opportunity is the ATV RiderCourse, a half-day, hands-on training program available to youths from 6 to 15 years of age, which is conducted only on ATVs of the appropriate size recommended for the rider's age. Kids between 12 and 15 are taught in classes limited to six students—and it's recommended that parents or guardians be present. Students between 6 and 11 are taught in classes limited to four people, and parents or guardians must be present. ATV Safety Institute (ASI)–licensed instructors evaluate the performance of all students during each lesson and provide the evaluation form to the student during the last lesson. The ATV RiderCourse is offered at 1,000 locations nationwide; for information, call 800-887-2887.

The final step is to not allow unsupervised use by youngsters. Just use plain common sense. Do not allow unsafe situations to occur. Youngsters don't always see danger and, of course, often don't understand.

An excellent booklet, *Parents, Youngsters and ATVs*, is available from the ASI. Additional information is available from local dealers, including a video titled *On Target, Off Road.* The ATV owner's manual provides warnings, cautions, and operating tips as well. It's also important to know local and state laws regarding the use of ATVs and youngsters.

With introducing a youngster to the fun of ATVs comes the responsibility of teaching proper environmental use and, when used in conjunction with hunting, following game rules and regulations. This provides a great tool for learning about the outdoors.

Youth-Model ATVs

Most manufacturers offer downsized models for youths. Polaris's line of kids' ATVs lets kids enjoy the same outdoor adventures as the rest of the family. Each of the company's youth-sized ATVs is a replica of its adult-sized counterpart, just a little smaller. For children ages 6 to 11, the new Scrambler 50 gives little ones a chance to explore the great outdoors. And their older siblings can hit the trails on their own Scrambler 90, or Sportsman 90, designed for riders aged 12 to 15.

All three youth models are stacked with safety features. Included in the purchase is a helmet, bright orange whip flag, and safety courses provided by Polaris dealers. Polaris youth models also feature electric starters, brake lights, and an adjustable throttle that allows parents to set the speed to the child's riding ability—all to make it easy, fun, and safe for children and teens to get out of the house and enjoy the outdoors with their family.

"We're committed to bringing the great outdoors to the entire family," says Mitchell Johnson, Polaris ATV division general manager. "By introducing a range of new products, we're giving people an opportunity to break their routines, have some fun together, and create out-of-the-ordinary adventures and experiences as a family."

Yamaha offers its Badger model for riders 12 and over and its Breeze version for those 16 and over. The Honda FourTrax 90 is recommended for riders 12 and up.

ATV and Off-Road Racing

Another exciting use of ATVs is off-road racing. A number of events are held around the country. For more information, contact the Grand National Cross Country at www.gnccracing.com.

Another exciting use of ATVs is off-road racing. A number of events are held across the country. (Photo courtesy Yamaha)

ATV RESPONSIBILITY

Not everyone enjoys ATVs in the outdoor scene. If someone has spent three hours hiking to a secluded spot, and arrives only to hear the snarling sound of someone on an ATV approaching from the opposite direction, he or she may get a bit testy.

With the use of ATVs comes responsibility. A recent meeting of ATV and utility vehicle manufacturers centered on the responsibility of the industry to police and help contain the problems ATVs can cause. We as ATV riders must do all we can to ensure that the sport continues and that we have access to places to ride. To do this, a number of programs have been put into effect to educate ATVers as well as the general public about riding courtesy, the environment, and political concerns.

Tread Lightly! was launched in 1985 by the USDA Forest Service to help protect public and private lands. To maximize its effectiveness, program responsibility was transferred to the private sector, making Tread Lightly! a not-for-profit organization. Protecting the great outdoors through education became the mission of Tread

With ATVing comes responsibility to the environment. Programs such as Tread Lightly! offer education on safe and environmentally friendly ATVing.

Lightly!; ensuring future responsible use of the land and water became their purpose.

Tread Lightly!'s message now reaches an international audience of outdoor recreationists, including ATVers. Through the services of Tread Lightly!, recreationists learn that opportunities to use the outdoors tomorrow depends on how they recreate today.

The message is simple. Preserve our environment. Make the commitment to follow Tread Lightly! principles.

T — Travel only where you and your vehicle are permitted by keeping to designated routes only. Never blaze your own trail.

R — Respect the rights of others, such as hikers and other recreationists.

E — Educate yourself by obtaining travel maps and regulations from public agencies, complying with signs and barriers, and asking permission to cross private property.

A — Avoid streams, lakeshores, meadows, muddy roads and trails, steep hillsides, and wildlife and livestock.

D — Drive and travel responsibly to protect the environment and preserve opportunities to enjoy recreation on wild lands.

Other commonsense rules should also be used when riding ATVs on public trails and grounds.

The first is the fact that noise annoys many other recreationists. Noise also doesn't equal horsepower. Insufficient back pressure can lead to loss of power, and can even cause engine damage. Maintain your exhaust system. A properly packed muffler is as important to performance as it is to sound control. Remember: More sound means less ground.

Second, make sure your spark arrestor is working correctly. Faulty spark arrestors can start wildfires; always check yours before heading into a brushy or forested area. If you're not sure about the condition of your spark arrestor, take your vehicle to someone who knows what kind of trouble to look for. A little extra care requires only a few minutes of your time, and it could save an entire forest.

Make sure you understand rules and regulations governing riding in specific public areas. Some areas limit the width of the vehicle on certain trails, and may have other regulations.

We are facing the possibility of numerous road closings on America's public lands. The responsible use of ATVs on these roads can help prevent some of these closings. In addition, the organization Americans for Responsible Recreational Access is a strong voice in the governmental decision-making process concerning public land access.

ATVs can also be misused, destroying the fragile environment and creating ill will among nonusers. As ATV riders, it's extremely important to be aware of these problems, be careful where and how the vehicles are used, and be courteous to other outdoor recreationists.

A number of pamphlets are available from Tread Lightly! including *Bridge to Your Future*; *Tread Lightly! Guide to Responsible Four Wheeling*; *Tread Lightly! Junior High Curriculum*; and *Tread Lightly! Science Manual*. For more information or to join Tread Lightly! and receive their window decal, product catalog, a copy of *Tread Lightly! Trails* quarterly newsletter with tips and other information, contact Tread Lightly!, Inc., 298 24th Street, Suite 325, Ogden, UT 84401; call 800-966-9900; or visit www.treadlightly.org.

CHAPTER 8

Specialized Uses

ATVs and utility vehicles have quickly become adapted to a number of specialized uses. With the wide variety of accessories and wide range of models available, it's hard to think of a chore or area where these vehicles can't be helpful.

WORK SITE

ATVs and especially utility vehicles are fast becoming major tools on many job sites. One of the most unusual uses is by B&M Roofing in Boulder, Colorado. The company uses Honda ATVs to speed work in replacing roofs dozens of stories up in the sky. President Conrad A. Kawulok says, "We've been using ATVs for about 10 years now on commercial flat roofs. We're using the ATVs to pull material dump carts to get the debris from one end of the project to the other end, where we're using a crane to off-load the debris. Typically we only have one or two locations along the edge of the building where we can take these materials off. We might have to move the material 300, 400, or maybe even 500 feet from one edge of the building to the other. So rather than having people manually pulling the carts, we have the ATV doing the work for us. They're very helpful, they save us a lot of work and trouble. They're easy to operate and they also save us a lot of time and money. The ATV does the work of two or three men and speeds up the whole process."

Another extremely popular vehicle for the work site is the Mule 520. Larger than a full-sized ATV but smaller than a compact pickup, the Mule 520 features long-lasting tires designed to provide an excellent grip on smooth surfaces such as tarmac, while minimizing

ATVs are used in lots of ways, including on the job site. (Photo courtesy Honda)

disturbance to turf. Its 882-pound vehicle capacity allows the Mule 520 to carry more than 350 pounds in the tilting cargo bed. Its compact overall dimensions and dry weight of 781 pounds allow it to be hauled to the job site in the cargo bed of a full-sized pickup truck. E-Z-GO and Club Car utility vehicles were both spawned from industrial models.

AGRICULTURE

ATVs and utility vehicles have become increasingly popular as agricultural tools for farmers and ranchers. Paul Aquillard, a rice farmer in Bunkie, Louisiana, says, "We use them for making drainage ditches in ricefields, where we can't get our water off by using tractors making drainage ditches. I think it improved our drainage almost 100 percent. We used to drain ricefields using tractors and men, and it'd take all day to drain a 100-acre ricefield. Today one man can pull out a 100-acre ricefield in about two and a half hours. They're very reliable, and they do the job. I'd hate to think I had to do any work on the farm without them."

Utility vehicles such as the Mule offer even more versatility on the job site, and handle other chores well. (Photo courtesy Kawasaki)

Pete Richmond of Atlas Peak Vineyards in Napa Valley, California, finds his Honda ATVs indispensable. "We have four ATVs," Richmond says. "We use them for irrigation, sampling vineyards, checking for insects. Generally they're used on a daily basis. We got them specifically because they make much more efficient use of our employees' time. We're able to cover ground much faster than we can walking, which is generally what we would have to do in the past. We also take the ATVs to places where we can't get other vehicles.

"We can cover 30 to 40 samples a day, whereas if we were to do it manually—that is, walking—we could only cover about 15 samples a day. Walking a field to check the irrigation system, we couldn't cover more than, say, 25 acres a day. With the ATV we can cover 200 acres a day."

John Barcroft, a cattle rancher in Beaver, Oregon, uses his ATVs for everything from fixing fences to rounding up cattle, even going to pick up the paper. "I don't know of anything that's quite as reliable, whether it's a pickup or tractor. These things just run constantly and I've never had any trouble. I've never been to a shop with it—just put gas and oil into it and go. I'm 77 and I wouldn't attempt to run my operation without one."

SEARCH AND RESCUE

Volunteers of the Mid-Carmel Valley Fire District in California have a Mule 2510 that they customized to serve as a search-and-rescue vehicle. Because it is smaller than a full-sized vehicle, it can be used to gain access to areas that are otherwise difficult to reach. The Essex Manufacturing Company custom-builds the Kawasaki Mule into a full-service firefighting unit and/or a search-and-rescue unit.

The rangers of Passamaquoddy Warden Service in Princeton, Maine, use their Honda ATV as part of their basic equipment for getting around areas where four-wheel drive or footwork just isn't practical. They've discovered the ATV is the fastest, most effective way to get there and provide help.

RURAL FIRE DEPARTMENTS

ATVs and utility vehicles such as the Essex-customized Mules are both excellent tools for rural fire departments. Equipped with a tank

ATVs and utility vehicles can be custom rigged with a variety of accessories to create search-and-rescue or rural fire department vehicles. ATVs are also great fire-fighting tools.

sprayer, an ATV can be used to create fire lines. A utility vehicle can also carry a sprayer, gear, and even personnel to the field as needed. Both vehicles can get to areas regular trucks can't reach.

LAW ENFORCEMENT

An increasing number of law enforcement agencies are discovering the uses of ATVs. They allow officers to get into areas inaccessible without foot, bicycle, or horse patrols. Officer Brad L. Kloepfer of the Redlands Police Department in Redlands, California, says, "We use the ATVs for a variety of off-road enforcement. We use it to do searches for lost subjects. We also use it to enforce off-road rules, such as closed areas, helmet usage, safety equipment, spark arrestors, and so on.

"Before we got the ATVs, if we searched an area that we couldn't get a vehicle into, it was done on foot. We called in all the reserves we could, we had a mounted posse and an old Willys Jeep that we used, but it just wasn't sufficient enough to get us where we needed to go. Until we obtained the ATVs, our off-road enforcement was

ATVs have become increasingly popular with many law enforcement agencies, including park rangers. (Photo courtesy Honda)

almost nonexistent. The ATVs work wonderfully out here. They handle excellently. And they withstand anything you put them through. We've never had one break down yet. The cost savings to the department using the ATVs versus the old ways of searching by manpower is unbelievable. The ATVs have made us more versatile and time efficient."

Wal-Mart, the nation's largest retailer, bought an entire fleet of Mule 550s for courtesy patrols in parking lots of many of their stores.

ENABLING THE PHYSICALLY HANDICAPPED

Randy Brown, a farmer in Osceola, Iowa, says, "I have an ATV because I'm a paraplegic. The machine means mobility for me, letting me get out and away from the house and off hard surfaces. I use it on my farm. I utilize it to do chores, work livestock—just a multitude of uses. I first got an ATV back in 1973. I was retired out of the Marine Corps into a wheelchair back in '72. And I'm not one to just sit around and watch things grow. I want to be out there doing something. The ATV is very simple, capable of being adapted to different physical limitations for an individual to have more mobility, and move freely within his lifestyle."

Ron Powell, a farmer in North Judson, Indiana, is another disabled person whose life is richer because of ATVs. His wife, Mary Kay Powell, says, "His neurological condition is called cerebellar ataxia, and he's been having difficulty walking since back in the '70s when he was using crutches. So he's used an ATV since that time. It gives him freedom that he would not have in any other way."

Ron uses the ATV to go about his farm and inspect things first-hand. It also gives him the option of doing it when he wants to and in the way he wants to. He isn't dependent upon someone else all the time. He uses the ATV for hauling straw and feed to the animals, and simply to get around.

WILDLIFE MANAGEMENT

ATVs have done their part in wildlife management, too. Marine biologist David Addison says, "When a turtle comes up and nests, we have a maximum of about 25 to 30 minutes to get to the nest to protect it with a cage before the raccoons get to it. So we need something that we know is going to do the job. We wouldn't be able to do the project without a means of getting up and down the beach with ATVs. We've got so many turtles nesting, you can't walk and carry the equipment that you need to protect all the nests. We have fallen logs and stuff, and you can't get around these things with a larger vehicle. And the ATV fits the bill: It's designed for this kind of work. We very seldom miss any nests now, because we're using these machines. From the standpoint of a biologist who's involved with a field project like this, the ATVs have enabled us to conduct this project in a reliable, cost-effective manner. And we've been able to protect a lot more sea turtle nests than we might otherwise have been able to."

Accessories

Utility vehicle and ATV accessories make up one of the fastest-growing outdoor industries. If you can think of it, someone is probably manufacturing it. If you can't think of it, someone else probably is. I've covered a number of accessories for hunting, groundbreaking, food-plot planting, and other uses in previous chapters. In addition to these products, most ATV manufacturers offer a full line of other accessories to fit their specific

Lots of accessories are available to add to your ATV and make it easier to use, more versatile, and suited to a variety of chores. (Photo courtesy Kawasaki)

machines. Most utility vehicle companies also sell gear to fit their vehicles. The following accessories can add to the usefulness, comfort, and productivity of your ATV and utility vehicle.

ATVs

Camouflage Kits

Many manufacturers offer either full-camouflaged models or kits to camouflage their models. The latter often consist of cloth coverings that snap or tie in place on the fenders, seat, and other areas of a specific unit. Custom seat and fender covers are available for ATVs from Cabela's and Bass Pro. These fit the most popular utility ATV models and are made of 500-denier Cordura, which is waterproof and scratch resistant. These seat and fender covers are available in Mossy Oak Break-Up. Also available are "decal" types such as Camoclad kits, which come in either removable or permanent applications from CDS, Inc. Bass Pro and Cabela's sell these kits in all the most popular camouflage patterns.

Although some ATVs are available with factory camouflage, a number of after—market camouflage kits are available to dress up your hunting vehicle and make it more concealable. (Photo courtesy Yamaha)

Polaris offers a full cloth covering in fluorescent orange for those who want extra protection in the woods during deer or turkey season. Also available from Polaris are matching cloth bags for front and rear racks.

Instant camouflage in the woods or marshes, plus weather protection for your ATV, can be had in the form of ATV covers from Walk-Winn, Avery Outdoors, Cabela's, Bass Pro, API Outdoors, and many ATV manufacturers.

Bags and Boxes

Innovative manufacturers have produced a wide variety of bags, boxes, and racks that can be used on ATVs to carry everything from your lunch to a chain saw. All the ATV manufacturers also carry their own aftermarket bags and boxes. The soft bags range from saddle style to fit over the seat to full-sized units that can be attached to front and rear racks. One I particularly liked on a long trail ride was the front bag from Yamaha, which has a clear plastic sleeve to hold a map in place in plain view, yet protected from the weather.

Lots of bags and soft packs are available to fit all over your ATV to help organize and carry different types of gear. (Photo courtesy Yamaha)

A number of hard cases, racks, and boxes, such as the rifle case shown make it easy to pack a lot of gear. (Photo courtesy Suzuki)

Several other companies also produce these handy soft packs, including API. Their Outdoors Ride N' Pack, which attaches to the rear cargo rack and has a 2- by 42-inch bottom cushion on which you can attach tree stands, coolers, and gun or bow cases. The API Pack N' Bag attaches to the front or rear rack and is a spacious 21 x 45 x 8-inch pouch for transporting anything from sleeping bags to tents and clothing. Cabela's also carries fender bags, contour utility bags, and their exclusive Backrest Bag, which keeps your gear stored and your back supported on long rides. IPI carries a full line of ATV bags as well.

When it comes to hard cases, there's just as much to choose from. A wide range of boxes is available from the various manufacturers. Several hard boxes are available from Cabela's and CDS, to name a few. Cabela's has several models, but their Motovan model has not only storage but also a padded seat and backrest to provide a place to rest when you're stopped. In addition to front and rear rack cases, CDS also has the Cajun Dri-Stor model that mounts off the back of the rear rack for additional storage, leaving the rear rack open. Tamarack Quad Trunks are easy to install and remove and provide water- and dust-free rear and front boxes for ATV racks. The rear box has up to 3 cubic feet of storage space and also provides a backrest. Cycle Country has two giant models that can fit on the back racks. They are quickly and easily attached with industrial-strength bungee cords.

Hard racks and baskets are also extremely popular. The Cabela's ATV Drop Basket Rack has an innovative drop feature at the rear that holds bulky items such as camping and hunting gear, or feed and seed bags. There's also space in the front of the rack for other gear. Cabela's has a flat basket rack for both front and rear. OxLite Manufacturing has a big detachable rear dolly basket that can also hold large items upright on the rear of the vehicle. The Cabela's exclusive ATV Hitch-Haul fits on the receiver hitch of your ATV and can be used for carrying a wide variety of bulky items. The Utility Rack Pad from CDS provides a nonskid surface for basket racks and is easily custom-fit for any rack.

Auxiliary Fuel and Water Packs

Cabela's ATV Fuel and Water Packs, which are stackable packs of polyethylene holding 3.28 gallons each, are extremely practical. They are designed flat so that you can strap them down on ATV racks, stacking them as needed. You can place both a fuel and water or more packs on top of each other and still have a place for

Auxiliary fuel, such as the Cajun Gas from CDS, Inc., increases your range and provides security on long rides. (Photo courtesy CDS, Inc.)

accessories such as gun racks. The fuel packs are red and have non-venting, easy-pour, anti-vibration caps. The water packs are white. CDS has a Cajun Auxiliary Gas Tank that allows gas lines to plug into a switch valve. It readily installs on either front or rear racks or off the rear rack.

Other Gear Gadgets

A number of accessories are available to hold a variety of tools for all types of chores. The Chain Saw Mount, from CDS, is a metal sleeve lined with plastic that will attach to any rack or basket. The CDS ATV Utility Rack holds long objects such as trimmers, shovels, and hoes and mounts inside the wheelbase of the ATV, so gear won't hang up on trees and shrubs. IPI also has a tool carrier that can hold both small and large items. Tool carriers are also available from Bass Pro and Cabela's.

The ATV Torch from Rugged Gear mounts to any ATV rack or bar and is easy to swivel up and down or around. It uses the ATV power source or a 12-volt plug. Cell phone mounts are available from IPI as well as Cabela's and Polaris. Polaris also offers Garmin III Plus GPS, in addition to a handlebar mount. The same company offers a handlebar cup holder and a video camera mount in case you wish to film your adventures.

Some ATVs come with hitches as standard; others utilize aftermarket receiver hitches that can be removed or installed as needed.

If you need to leave your ATV in the woods in an unprotected area, the Cabela's Club 7-foot Cable Lock can be used to padlock your vehicle to a tree, trailer, or other solid object. Yellow vinyl coating deters thieves and protects your ATV from scratches.

Performance Accessories

Tires and Wheels

Changing tires to larger sizes or different types of treads is one of the most common upgrades ATV owners make. The different tire sizes and treads do affect handling and performance, however. The larger, heavier, and more aggressive the tire, the more horsepower required. Also, larger-diameter tires create less gear ratio, and therefore lessen power. Experts consider the engine size in ratio to the tire size.

The 250cc ATVs should be limited to 22-inch tires. The 300 to 350cc ATVs can handle up to 25-inch tires, the 400 to 450cc ATVs can handle 26-inch tires, and the 500 to 600cc units can handle the large 27-inch tires. Industrial Tire Products carries a full line of high-quality Blackwater tires, including 26- and 27-inchers. They also sell complete bolt-on kits with tires mounted on ITP steel wheels. Each BigWheel Kit is specifically designed to enhance the ability of the ATV for which it is intended. The kits offer greatly increased traction, flotation, and ground clearance compared with OEM products.

If you're into mudding, the ultimate mud tire setup is the Swamp King from ITP. This provides maximum traction and flotation for the front end, although it's not recommended for everyday trail usage. Also available are AG kits featuring tires designed specifically for very wet farming conditions. These tires can turn 4x4 ATVs into "tractors." The tires have four-ply, self-cleaning superlug treads for slow-speed agricultural usage. The narrow tires dig deep and find traction where others can't. Polaris also offers a full line of pure Polaris replacement tires for a variety of uses, as does Arctic Cat.

You may wish to upgrade original equipment tires if you do mudding or use your ATV mostly for food plots and other agricultural chores.

Lift Kits

Lift kits are often used in areas where deep mud or wet snow can be a problem for deer and waterfowl hunters. Lift kits typically raise the front of the vehicle about 2 inches. The only way you can lift the rear is with larger tires. A lift kit in conjunction with oversized tires and wheels can add about 4 inches to the height of the vehicle. Remember, however, that the added height and ground clearance will alter the performance and handling. More care must be taken in hill climbing due to the increased height and balance of the machine.

The High Lifter Products lift kits are made for most modern utility ATVs and are a system of bolt-on brackets that require no welding, cutting, or drilling to install.

Performance Kits

You can also purchase entire performance kits. The Bad to the Bone package from High Lifter includes Super Swamper Vampire Tires, Douglas aluminum wheels, a 2-inch High Lifter Lift Kit, an ATV Locker (for true 4WD), off-road floorboards, a heavy-duty front skid plate, a Monster Power High Performance Kit including Super-Trapp IDS Quiet Series exhaust system, a Dynojet Jet Kit, a K&N High Flow air filter, an NGK Platinum Tip Performance Spark Plug, a water-resistant prefilter, a supplemental air breather hose (optional for some models), and a performance cam (optional for some models).

Thumb Shifts

The ElectriXShift from Cycle Country allows you to shift with your thumb rather than your foot on vehicles with foot shifts. This is especially handy when you're riding standing up. The unit allows your stock shifter to remain in place. The ElectriXShift features a 12-volt DC motor driven by state-of-the-art electronics. The microprocessor ensures fast, precise shifting.

Thumb Throttle Controls

On the other side of the handlebars is the standard ATV throttle. Over a long day's ride, your thumb inevitably becomes cramped. The CDS Thumb Saver is a throttle extension that takes the pressure off that digit. The Thumb Saver is made of durable, molded plastic and fits all models of ATVs. With the Thumb Saver, you can use the palm of your hand or your thumb to control the throttle.

ATV Protective Gear

Some of the most popular performance accessories include skid plates that protect the bottom of engine cases and frame tubes from heavy blows. These are available for most of the popular utility ATVs from the various manufacturers, as well as from Cabela's. Also available are CV boot guards from many manufacturers. The ATV Stick Stopper Plates from Cabela's protect the most vulnerable joints, which are normally protected only by rubber boots.

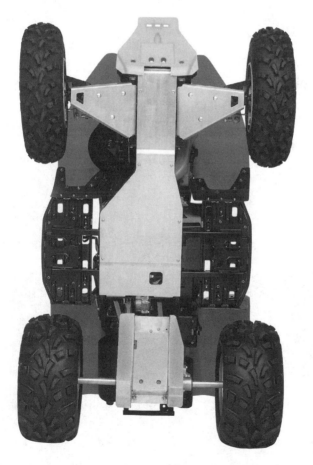

Skid plates and other protective gear are offered after market by many ATV and accessory manufacturers to provide more protection in off-road use. (Photo courtesy Polaris)

Protective Gear for Riders

All the major ATV manufacturers offer some sort of protective gear, from clothing to gloves to fairings, for their vehicles. Both the latter are also available from Cabela's, as is a full cab enclosure. Made of ultratough nylon, the cab enclosure keeps the elements outside without restricting visibility. The Weathermaster ATV enclosure from Cabela's features an ABS plastic roof, no-rust aluminum frame, double rear crossbars, seat belts, molded Lexan enclosure, and hinged front access panel. Optional features include rear storage rack, removable rain flaps, and a gun rack.

UTILITY VEHICLES

Camouflage Kits

Camouflage kits are available for most utility vehicles, most in cloth that can fit over the fenders, seats, and other areas. I rigged a Mule as a pure hunting vehicle utilizing a Realtree camouflage kit from

Utility vehicles also have a lot of accessories that can be added. (Photo courtesy Polaris)

Utility vehicles also have available a variety of camouflage kits such as the Mule camo kit from Kawasaki.

Kawasaki. The kit contained a number of pieces to camouflage the vehicle fully, including a full set of bed side covers held in place with hook-and-loop strips, heavy-duty seat covers for both the seat bottom and back, hook-and-loop covers for the roll cage front bars, and a full top cover. The latter features a vinyl back and side curtain and a ripstop cloth top that provides shade and comfort as well as some protection from bad weather.

A specially designed cowling cover that covered the front of the vehicle, the dash, and down the fender sides of the front was also included. The Realtree camouflage rigging makes it easy to park the vehicle close to a duck blind or hide it in the woods near a deer stand. Wheel covers were even included in the kit to cover the shiny wheel rims and tires. The kit is extremely well made and sturdy enough to last for a long time in the woods.

Enclosures

The Mule and Polaris Ranger models come standard with cage bars, while most of the other units also have bars as an option. One of the most common accessories is a top or cover to fit over the frames. Another popular gadget is a windshield, available in whole or split models. An option for the frame is a light bar that fastens on the top and can be used for cargo lighting, with fog lamps or as additional driving lights.

Some models, such as the Mules, E-Z-GO WorkHorse, and Club Car Pioneer models, come with soft-sided enclosures to fit over the cage bars and provide full protection from the weather. The Mule comes with a wide range of hard-sided enclosures, complete with windshield wipers, heater, and other cold-weather necessities. All of these are available from Kawasaki.

The Mule has the largest lineup of accessories, available from both Kawasaki and Essex Manufacturing, Inc., which makes a full line of accessories for the Mule, including complete kits that provide more comfort and better performance. The Complete Safari kit, for example, includes a steel cab with dome light and accessory harness; lift windshield; steel doors with slider back window; cab heater; suspension lift kit and Blackwater 27-inch tires; spare tire mounted on a front basket; heavy-duty bumper; Warn Winch with

Windshields are extremely popular with utility vehicle owners, and may be one or two piece, or fold-down. (Photo courtesy Yamaha)

Soft enclosures are also available for some models. (Photo courtesy E-Z-GO)

The Mule comes with the largest lineup of accessories, including complete hard-enclosure kits, as well as accessories to utilize the bed in any number of ways.

handheld remote controller; bed extension to 58 inches, including a rear bumper or foldaway step; CV boot guards; and engine skid plate. Options to the kit include a cabin accessory packet with rearview and exterior mirrors, floor mats, floorpan, and sound package; 12-volt power ports and two-speed fan; and halogen headlights and harness for bed lights. The bed can be further customized with a high seat for two people; two-, four-, and six-compartment dog boxes with seating; gun mounts and rests; a shooter's cart; and a foldaway bed step for access to seats or cargo.

Essex can also custom-build the Mule to fit almost any situation, including a shooter's cart for hunting preserves; a bird dog box; a firefighting unit; a multipurpose fire unit with storage compartment for rescue gear; and an all-weather cargo outfit to protect the cargo. Essex even makes a special 78-inch extended bed for use in cemeteries and other unique situations.

While field testing a Mule, I tried out the Cycle Country bed lift kit, an electromechanical screw-driven lift kit that easily lifts the tilt bed without the use of leaky hydraulics. If you fill the beds of many of these units with rocks or firewood, you won't be able to lift them for dumping. The bed lift kit's electric assist is invaluable.

Club Car has a full hard cab as well. (Photo courtesy Club Car)

For the hunting Mule version, I bolted on a mini vault from Advanced Security Products. This is perfect for safely carrying a handgun on the Mule. It features a 16-gauge steel housing with fittings so precise that it's virtually impossible to open with any hand tool. The unit also has a patented No-Eyes keypad entry that allows you to simply lay your hand in place and tap with your fingers the personal access code for instant access. A motion detector alarm is also a feature.

Club Car Pioneer units also have a full hard cab enclosure with either soft or steel doors, as well as a cab heater, inside dome light, glove box, outside mirrors, cab fan/defogger, and rear fold-down seat for the cargo area as options.

E-Z-GO has a one-piece and fold-down windshield, light bar with beacon, all-weather enclosure, rearview mirror, right- and left-hand locking glove boxes, and turn signals with four-way flasher as options.

The cargo beds of many utility ATVs can be customized with tool boxes from Kawasaki, E-Z-GO, and Club Car. Kawasaki and Club Car also offer stake side kits to increase the carrying capacity of their cargo beds.

Many ATVs and utility vehicles can be fitted with snow blades or even snow throwers. (Photo courtesy Polaris)

ATV AND UTILITY ACCESSORIES

A number of accessories can be used on both ATVs and utility vehicles.

Snow Blades

Both ATVs and utility vehicles can be fitted with snow blades. Cabela's carries a Motorsports ATV plow, while Cycle Country has blades for both ATVs and utility vehicles, as do Polaris and Kawasaki. These front-mounted blades can be used as snowplows or for light grading work, cleaning trails, and other chores. Polaris also has a front-mounted snow blower.

Chore Aids

Polaris has a pull-behind sweep that collects debris in its 42-inch-wide, 12-cubic-foot-capacity hopper, which can be raised for dumping

Straight blades are also available for ATV and utility vehicles. (Photos courtesy Yamaha)

Sweepers and other accessories are also available from Polaris. (Photo courtesy Polaris)

and lowered again by the driver without leaving the seat. The Sweeper uses a 6.5-horsepower Briggs and Stratton engine. It swivels for angled sweeping and is great for cleaning up dirt, snow, leaves, and work site debris.

You can even use your ATV as a forklift with an accessory from Weekend Warrior. (Photo courtesy Weekend Warrior)

One of the more unusual accessories is the new forklift from Weekend Warrior. It mounts on the front of the vehicle, and if you need to pick up and move heavy equipment, rocks, tools, or even downed game, it can handle these tasks quite easily.

Chains, Tracks, and Skis

Chains to fit OEM tires are available from most manufacturers. These can provide added traction in ice and snow or for pulling chores such as skidding out logs or pulling groundbreaking implements. ICC, a division of Wallingford's, offers their Super Stud chain models with two studs on every other link for even greater traction.

For the ultimate in traction, Polaris offers 6x6 tracks that can turn your Sportsman 6x6 or Big Boss 6x6 off-road vehicle into a "swamp thing." These tracks provide superior flotation and go where other ATVs fear to tread. They're great for snow as well.

Polaris also has skis that fit over trailer wheels, allowing utility trailers to be used on ice and snow. The steel skis have replaceable wear rods and fully adjustable straps, buckles, and side bar to ensure a secure fit on tires from 8 to 15 inches.

If your thing is swamps, you might consider the Polaris 6x6 with accessory tracks. (Photo courtesy Polaris)

Getting Unstuck

A TV stands for "all-terrain vehicle," which means you can go through all types of terrain. Just like your first four-wheel-drive truck or SUV, however, you'll eventually discover you can get an ATV stuck. And when you do, it's messy. Usually you're in a spot where you can't get another vehicle to the ATV to pull it out. One simple tool can usually solve this problem, however—a winch mounted on the front of your ATV.

Sooner or later you're going to get stuck. That's when you'll want an ATV-mounted winch. (Photo courtesy Polaris)

The ATV-mounted winch can be used for numerous other hunting and outdoor chores as well. A deer or big-game carcass down in a ravine or other spot that is too unsafe to access with the ATV can be extricated with the winch. Back at camp, the same winch can be used to hoist the carcass up to a meat pole or tree limb for skinning and butchering. Got a downed tree in your woods that you want to haul back to camp for firewood? If you can't get to the tree because of dense woods, winch it out.

ATV WINCHES

Winches are available as accessory items from most ATV manufacturers, or as aftermarket items. Warn Industries ATV winches are available in two sizes: the A2500, which has a remote control pack; and the A2000, which utilizes a direct switch mounted on the ATV. A steel hawse-style fairhead is included to increase wire rope life. The Rule 14 and 20 Series winches are ideally suited for ATVs or as small utility winches. They feature compact design, come with freespool, and are available with 25 or 50 feet of cable. Roller heads and remote mounting kits are available as accessories. Hi-Per Sports sells aftermarket winches, as do Cycle Country and Bass

ATV winches are available from most ATV manufacturers, or from after-market manufacturers. Make sure you get a unit made for ATVs.

Pro. Cabela's carries Trail Tamer ATV winches from SuperWinch, including their 1500 and 2000 models.

It's important to use a winch designed for an ATV instead of an automotive model. Pull ratings of the various winches are in pounds, with the maximum pulling power in the first roll of cable on the drum. As you increase the number of layers, the pull rating decreases.

Your ATV dealer can mount the winch, or you can mount it yourself. If you do it yourself, follow the manufacturer's mounting instructions explicitly. Cutting corners during mounting can create a dangerous situation. A fairhead roller should also be mounted in conjunction with the winch to provide easier load handling.

RIGGING WINCHES

Winches can be rigged in three different methods. The first is straight-line, single-pull rigging. In this case, the cable is directed in a straight line to an anchor from the front of the ATV. Always spool out as much wire rope as possible when preparing rigging. Pick an anchor as far away as possible. This provides the winch with its greatest pulling power.

The second method is direction-change pull. If you can't get a straight-line pull with a single anchor, you can use a snatch block and two anchors to rig a direction-change pull. This allows you to

Single-line pull

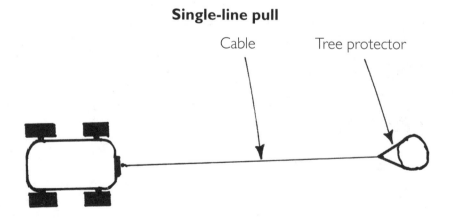

Winches can be rigged several ways. Straight line pull is most commonly used.

Direction Change

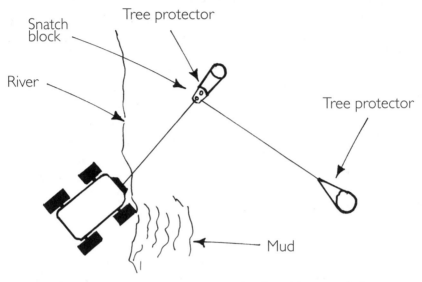

By changing direction of the pull, you can route the cable as needed.

Single-line pull

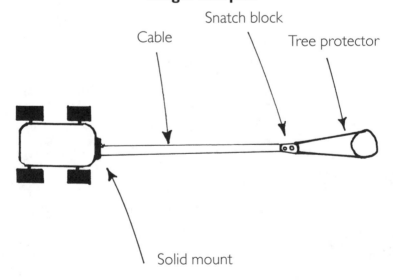

A double-line, straight-line pull offers tremendous pulling power.

route the winch cable to create an angle for the pull, but still allow the cable to wind straight on the winch.

For more power, use the third method, a double-line, straight-line pull with a snatch block located at the anchor. This does reduce line speed, however. In a really serious case, you can create even more pulling power by using two snatch blocks and two anchor points. A tremendous pull can be exerted using these tactics. Make sure the cable is in good shape and the snatch blocks of good quality. The cable should be anchored with bow shackles.

CHOOSING ANCHORS

Natural anchors such as trees, stumps, and rocks are the handiest when available. When using a tree as the anchor, make sure the tree will be able to take the pressure, and use a tree trunk protector. This provides a point to attach the shackle and wire hook and also protects the tree trunk. Attach the choker chain, wire choker rope, or tree trunk protector on the anchor as low as possible to avoid pulling the anchor down. If several possible anchors are available, but none is strong enough individually, you may be able to attach a wire or chain choker around several anchors to form a strong collective anchor point.

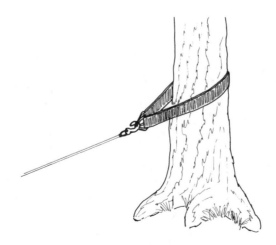

Make sure you use a good solid anchor; if the anchor is a tree, use a protector for the trunk so you don't scar it with the cable.

Unspooling

Before using a new wire rope, unspool, leaving five wraps on the drum. Then power in the wire rope under a load of at least 500 pounds. This will stretch the new rope and create a good wrap around the drum. Failure to do so can result in the outer wire wraps drawing into the inner wraps, binding and damaging the wire rope.

If possible, make the pull straight to minimize binding or loading of the cable on one side of the drum and to ensure maximum line pull capacity. Never winch with less than five coils of wire rope left on the drum. This prevents the possibility of the line coming loose. Take up the slack in the rope by pulsing the switch to avoid shock loads when the line becomes taut. Always monitor the heat of the winch motor on long pulls by occasionally touching the motor. If it becomes hot to the touch, turn it off and allow it to cool for a few minutes.

Respooling

To respool the winch after use, have an assistant walk the rope back, providing some pressure on the rope. If you are without an assistant, make sure the rope isn't kinked or uneven as it respools.

Winch Safety

Follow all safety rules when using winches and wire rope. Lay a blanket or heavy jacket over the cable about midpoint to reduce the velocity if the cable should break. Don't allow anyone to step over the cable. Keep all bystanders away at least one and a half times the length of the paid-out cable. Always wear gloves when working with wire rope.

A winch can be invaluable to ATVers in the backcountry as well as around camp. Knowing how to use the winch before it is actually needed is even more invaluable.

11

Transporting ATVs

S afely and easily transporting your ATV to a favorite hunting, fishing, camping, or riding site is a very important aspect of ATVing. Transporting usually means using an open pickup bed or some sort of trailer. As with most of the ATV market, a growing number of products are available for transporting ATVs.

PICKUP TRANSPORT

If you have a pickup that your ATV will fit into, a number of ramps let you drive the vehicle up into the pickup bed. Make sure the pickup is suitable for hauling the weight and size of the ATV. Your most economical choices are ATV ramp kits, which include a pair of extruded aluminum ramp tops that you mount to 2 x 8-inch planks. It does take some skill in driving up these ramps, and they must be precisely positioned. I've been using an API aluminum loading ramp for some time; it's extremely lightweight and folds to fit between the ATV wheels while the machine is in the back of my truck. The ramps are rather short, with a steep drive up. A longer, trifold model is now available that is easier and safer to use. All are sold by Bass Pro and Cabela's.

Cabela's also carries heavy-duty loading ramps of the same style as well as several longer, folding loading ramps. Many manufacturers also offer ramps for loading ATVs into either pickup beds or trailers. OxLite Manufacturing has a full line of ramps including bipanel hinged, tripanel hinged, single runners, collapsing runners, and dual runners. It's a good idea to use arched ramps for lower-clearance machinery so you don't risk catching the vehicle on the drop-over from the ramp into the transport area.

Transporting ATVs is often an important part of their use. ATVs and some utility vehicles can be transported in the back of a pickup. A number of loading ramps are available for driving the ATVs into place.

Securing your ATV in the pickup is easy with the Louisiana Guard Dog ATV securing device. No straps, no bouncing. The device fits into your truck hitch and swings away quickly for loading and unloading. The device also prevents the ATV from sliding forward if your truck is in a front-end vehicle accident. If you want to use your pickup for other purposes or have a heavy-duty SUV, consider the Carry-All, a wheel-less trailer that fits into the receiver tube of a Class III hitch. The Carry-All tilts down to load easily and is available from the Northern Tool & Equipment Company catalog.

TRAILERS

Another alternative is a trailer that can be used to transport the ATVs as well as other gear. Many ATV dealers carry utility trailers for this purpose. Most have built-in ramps that drop down for loading, then swing up to secure the ATV. Polaris has a full line of trailers, including their open flat-bed tilt and ramp models. The tilt model

The Louisiana Guard Dog ATV securing device makes it easy to secure the unit in place, and prevents it from sliding forward in case of an accident.

features a fast-action clamp for ease of operation and elimination of rattles and vibration. The ramp version allows ramps to be used. Both versions are available in 9- and 12-foot lengths. All of these trailers can also serve double duty as utility trailers around the farm and home. Polaris also has a fully enclosed trailer to make trailering easy and provide more protection for your investment.

Many utility vehicles are too wide for the smaller ATV trailers. A standard 5- or 6-foot-wide utility trailer solves that problem easily. I have such a trailer fitted with drive-on ramps and use it for hauling everything from ATVs to utility vehicles, tractors, and implements.

If the trailer is lightweight, you can fit a ball hitch on your ATV and use the trailer at the hunting site to haul wood, carry your game out of the woods, and perform other chores. An excellent model is available from Weekend Warrior. Triton also carries a line of excellent all-aluminum, lightweight trailers.

The Magenta Utility Tilt Trailer lets you load or off-load your ATV on virtually any terrain without ramps because the bed tilts. The Magenta holds up to 1,500 pounds and can be towed behind

Trailers are also often used for transporting ATVs; a number are designed just for that purpose, with drive-on ramps included.

an ATV. Stake pockets allow you to custom-build side boards and end gates if desired. The trailer bed accepts a 4 x 8 sheet of 0.75-inch plywood (not included) to complete.

ATV trailer locks that can be attached to the floor of the trailer to secure the unit in place are available from several manufacturers. Pingel ATV wheel chocks can also be used to secure an ATV in a trailer or pickup. I use ratchet-style tiedowns on all four corners to make sure the unit stays safely in place.

BEFORE TRANSPORTING

1. Turn off the engine and remove the key. It may be lost or stolen if not removed.
2. Turn off the fuel valve.
3. Make certain the fuel cap, oil cap, seat, and any accessories are installed correctly and not loose.
4. Always tie the frame of the ATV to the transporting unit securely, using suitable straps or rope.
5. Always place the transmission in gear and lock the parking brake.

SAFETY RULES

Regardless of the method of transporting, but especially when using ramps to load an ATV on higher vehicles, it's extremely important to follow all safety rules. Do not exceed the maximum weight limits of any ATV loading ramp as specified by the manufacturer. This includes the combined weight of the operator and the ATV. Make sure the ramp is properly prepared and secured to the vehicle as per the manufacturer's instructions. Wear a safety helmet!

LOADING AND UNLOADING

Place the four-wheel ATV in low range and/or first gear and drive it slowly onto the ramp. Check to make sure the unit is centered with the loading ramp. At this point, lean forward slightly and accelerate just enough to proceed up the ramp. This may take a bit of practice. Once the four-wheeler is in the truck or trailer bed, engage

It's important to follow all safety rules when driving ATVs up ramps, including wearing a helmet.

the brakes. For additional security and safe transporting, the unit should be secured to the truck bed with tiedowns or some other means of fastening.

To unload, secure the ramps properly as for loading. Wear a safety helmet. Unlock the brakes and, with the four-wheeler in low range and/or reverse, slowly back up until the ATV is at the point it will free-roll down the ramp. Do not apply any throttle while backing down the ramp. Once all four wheels are on the ground, you can apply throttle.

With the right means of transportation, your ATV can be a doorway to tremendous hunting, fishing, camping, and riding opportunities.

Maintenance

Today's ATVs are rugged, long-lasting, and efficient machines. They do require regular maintenance, however. The first step is to thoroughly read your owner's manual regarding the regime your specific vehicle requires. Although some steps are fairly common among all ATVs, other steps will vary according to type. Some ATVs require minimal maintenance, others a bit more.

You don't need many tools for most maintenance chores, although those you use should precisely fit the nuts, bolts, and

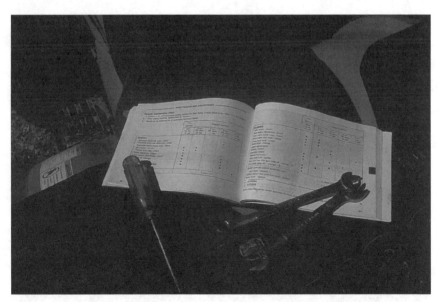

ATVs require regular maintenance. Follow the maintenance schedule outlined in the owner's manual.

fittings of your particular unit. Use only the oil and grease specified by your manufacturer.

DAILY WALK-AROUND INSPECTION

Before you begin each day's ride, make a habit of doing a "walk-around" inspection. This short daily checkup can prolong the life of your vehicle—and maybe your own.

- Check to make sure enough fuel is in the tank for the activities you have planned and that there are no fuel leaks.
- Make sure the fuel vent hose is free, not kinked.
- Check the oil level.
- Check air pressure of the tires (when cold) and inflate them according to tire manufacturer's specifications.
- Check the air cleaner element, and clean it if necessary. This is one of the most important maintenance checks—a dirty filter can shorten the life of your engine.

Make it a point to inspect your vehicle before every ride. (Photo courtesy Yamaha)

- Check all nuts, bolts, and fasteners. Pay special attention to the wheel nuts, hub nuts, stem bearing bracket bolts, front and rear rack mounting bolts, brake lever pivot nut, and brake level holder screws, as well as the suspension arm pivot bolts, muffler mounting bolts, throttle case screws, brake master cylinder clamp bolts, and exhaust pipe holder nuts. It doesn't hurt to place a few drops of oil occasionally on the bolts and nuts to prevent rusting and sticking.
- Make sure that the steering and suspension components, axles, and all controls are properly fastened in place. Vibration can eventually cause these to loosen, and a loose control on a steep downhill run can be disastrous. Especially check that the steering is not overly loose from lock to lock, and that the control cables are not binding in any manner. Shake or twist the wheels from side to side to check for any looseness.
- Check for brake fluid leakage and make sure the brake pedals have the proper amount of free play according to the manufacturer's instructions.

Check the brakes. Watch for brake fluid leakage.

Check front and rear gear cases.

One of the most important maintenance tasks is cleaning the engine air cleaner or filter.

- Make sure the brakes work properly, and that the parking brake stops the vehicle immediately.
- Be sure the throttle lever has a specific amount of free play according to the manufacturer's specifications. It should snap back when released.
- The front and rear gear cases should be checked to ensure no oil is leaking.
- Turn on the lights and check that all work.
- Make sure the engine stop switch works.

REGULAR MAINTENANCE

After your ATV's first 10 hours of use, and every seven days of use after that, check the engine air cleaner, throttle lever play, brake adjustment, fuel system cleanliness, battery, steering, all bolts and nuts, transmission, and front and rear gear case oil.

It's also a good idea to clean the unit thoroughly from top to bottom at this time. Not only does washing keep your ATV looking better, but it also allows you to spot minor problems before

Wash the unit so you can easily see any problems that may occur.

they can become serious. Actually, anytime your ATV has been in saltwater, or operated on rainy days or in muddy or dusty conditions, it should be thoroughly cleaned. A high-pressure washer can make the task fast and easy, but most manufacturers do not recommend their use—especially coin-operated high-pressure washers—as the water may be forced into bearings and other components. Before washing, first cover the rear opening of the muffler with a plastic bag secured with a rubber band. Cover the brake levers, switch cases, and throttle case with plastic bags, and protect the ignition switch and keyhole with tape. Close the opening to the air intake with tape or stuff in rags. While washing, avoid spraying water with great force near the disc brake master cylinder or caliper, rear brake, and under the fuel tank.

After washing, remove all coverings and lubricate areas suggested by your manufacturer. Generally this means applying motor oil to the brake lever, brake cable joint, brake cam lever, and brake pedal. Grease should be applied to the upper end of the throttle's inner cable, and pressure cable lube should be applied to the rear brake inner cable and the throttle inner cable. Test the brakes before operating and then start the engine and run it for about five minutes.

After every 30 days of use, check the brake fluid level and the battery fluid levels, and do an overall lubrication.

After every 90 days of use, change the engine oil and oil filter as well as clean and gap the spark plug. Lubricate all fittings, pivots, and cables.

Every six months, check and change the engine oil and oil filter on four-cycle engines. On two-cycle engines, inspect, adjust, and lubricate the oil pump cable, and replace if required. Inspect the engine breather hose. Drain the carburetor bowl. Inspect the coolant. Check the front hub fluids on 4WD models. Inspect and adjust the shift linkage. Inspect the drive belt if the machine has one, and replace it if necessary. Inspect the steering and lubricate. Inspect the bearings and lubricate the rear axle as needed. Inspect, lubricate, and tighten front fasteners on both rear and front suspension. Inspect drive chains, adjust, and lubricate if needed.

After 12 months, inspect the radiator and clean the external surface. Inspect the cooling system hoses. You should also change the front and rear gear case oil.

It's extremely important to maintain the exhaust and spark arrestor.

Exhaust and Spark Arrestor

Check the exhaust system to make sure it is working properly. After each year of use, and before going on major trail rides, you should clean the spark arrestor. Although the techniques are basically the same regardless of the vehicle, make sure you follow your owner's manual for specifics on your particular ATV.

To clean the spark arrestor, in most instances you merely remove the cleanout plug or plugs located on the bottom of the muffler, and run the engine. First, a few safety rules. Do not perform this operation immediately after running the engine; the exhaust system can be very hot. Make sure there are no combustible materials in the area when purging the spark arrestor. Wear eye protection. Do not stand behind or in front of the vehicle while purging the carbon from the spark arrestor. Never run the engine in an enclosed area, as the exhaust contains carbon monoxide. Do not go under the machine while it is inclined. Keep combustible materials away from the exhaust system—fire may result.

Follow these steps to maintain your spark arrestor:
1. Remove the plug or plugs.
2. Place the transmission in neutral and start the engine.
3. Rev up the engine several times to purge the accumulated carbon from the system.
4. If some carbon is expelled, cover the exhaust outlet and rap on the pipe around the cleanout plugs while revving the engine several more times.
5. If you suspect that more particles are in the muffler, back the machine onto an incline so the rear of the machine is 1 foot higher than the front. Set the parking brake, make sure the machine is in neutral, then repeat steps 1 through 4.
6. If particles are still in the muffler, drive the machine onto the incline with the front higher than the rear. Set the parking brake and repeat steps 1 through 4 until no more particles are expelled when the engine is revved.
7. Shut down the engine and allow the arrestor to cool.
8. Reinstall the arrestor plugs.

If storing for the off-season, follow the manufacturer's instructions and use as a gasoline stabilizer.

STORAGE

Properly storing your unit during the off-season not only protects the unit and prolongs its life, but also makes starting at the beginning of the season easier. Following are storage tips from Polaris for their units.

- Clean the outside. Make necessary repairs and then clean the ATV thoroughly with a mild soap-and-warm-water solution to remove all dirt and grime. Don't use harsh detergents or high-pressure washers. Some detergents deteriorate rubber parts—use dish-soap-type cleaners only. High-pressure washers may force water past seals. Drain the recoil housing.
- Stabilize the fuel. Fill the fuel tank. Add Polaris Carbo Clean Fuel Treatment or Polaris Fuel Stabilizer. Follow instructions on the container for the recommended amount. Carbon Clean will reduce the possibility of bacterial growth in the fuel system. It's best to allow 15 to 20 minutes of operation for the stabilizer to disperse through the fuel in the tank and carburetor. Turn the fuel valve to off and drain the carburetor bowl completely.
- Oil and filter change (for four-stroke models). Warm the engine and change the oil and filter.
- Air filter/air box. Inspect and clean or replace the breather filter(s).
- Inspect all fluid levels and change if necessary: engine counterbalance (two-stroke models); front gear case (shaft-drive models); transmission; front hubs (4WD models); and brake fluid (change every two years or as required if fluid looks dark or contaminated).
- Drain the recoil housing. Remove the drain plug from the recoil housing and drain any moisture present.
- Fog the engine. For two-stroke engines, use Polaris Fogging Oil and follow directions on the can. For four-stroke engines, remove the spark plug and add 2 to 3 tablespoons of Premium 4 Synthetic 10W40 engine oil. To access the plug hose, use a section of clear 0.25-inch hose and a small plastic squeeze bottle filled with a premeasured amount of oil. Do this carefully! If you miss the plug hole, oil will drain from the spark plug cavity out of the hole at the front of the cylinder head, and appear to be an oil leak. Install the spark plug and

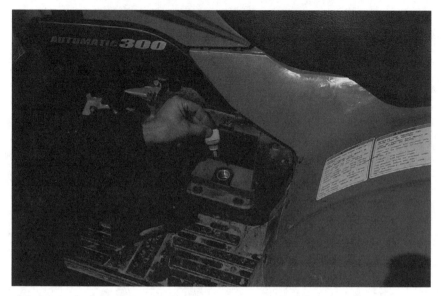

Lubricate and change engine oil and gear oils as needed before storing.

pull the engine over slowly with the recoil starter. Oil will be forced in and around the piston rings and ring lands, coating the cylinder with a protective film of fresh oil.

- Check and lubricate/grease the cables. Inspect all cables and lubricate with Polaris Cable Lubricant. Follow lubrication guidelines in the maintenance section of the service or owner's manual to completely grease and lubricate the entire vehicle with Polaris Premium All-Season Grease. Apply Polaris O-Ring Chain Lube to the drive chain(s).

- Perform battery maintenance. Remove the battery and add distilled water as required to the proper level. Do not use tap water, which may contain minerals that reduce battery life. Apply Polaris Di-Electric Grease to the terminal bolts and terminals. Charge the battery at 1.4 amps or less until specific gravity of each cell is 1.265 or greater. Store the battery in a cool, dry place. Charge can be maintained easily by using a Polaris Battery Tender charger or by charging about once a month to account for normal self-discharge. The Battery Tender can be left connected during the storage period and will automatically charge the battery if the voltage drops below a predetermined point. The only thing you need to do is check the fluid level once a month.

- Check the engine antifreeze. Test engine coolant strength and change if necessary. Coolant should be replaced every two years.
- Storage area/covers. Set the tire pressure, and safely support the ATV with the tires 1 to 2 inches off the ground. Be sure the storage area is well ventilated. Cover the machine with a genuine Polaris ATV cover. Do not use plastic or coated materials. They do not allow enough ventilation to prevent condensation, and may promote corrosion and oxidation.
- Do not start the engine during the storage period. This will disturb the protective film created by fogging.

ATV TIRE CARE

Half a day's ride from the nearest road, overnight camping on a mountaintop in Utah, and the first thing the morning brings is a flat tire on my ATV. No problem for Russ Brennan with Kawasaki. He whips out his handy off-road tool kit, plugs the hole with a tire plug, then pumps the tire back up with a hand pump. Actually, I was traveling with a group of half a dozen riders on the famous Paiute ATV Trail, and Brennan was prepared for anything. He was even carrying a couple of spare tires in case a real problem developed, such as a slash by a sharp Utah rock. If you're heading off-road, you should carry a tire repair kit. If you'll be in extremely rough backcountry, it's not a bad idea to carry a spare tire as well.

Flat Tires

A flat on an ATV can be a minor frustration or a serious problem, depending on where you are when it happens, what you have with you to fix it, and how bad the tire problem is. Large slashes will require professional repair, or maybe even tire replacement. Small punctures, however, such as those from nails, thorns, and sharp rocks, can often be repaired on the spot with plug kits available at automobile parts stores. You'll also need a bicycle hand pump or 12-volt accessory air pump if your ATV has an accessory plug.

Keep a tire plug kit on hand for repairing tires, and maintain proper air pressure as per your owner's manual.

Remove the object that caused the puncture. Insert the plug kit rasp into the hole and slide it up and down to roughen and clean the inside of the hole. Coat the plug kit needle with tire cement lubricant and slide it in and out of the hole to lubricate the hole. Insert the repair material in the needle, coat it thoroughly with cement, and insert the needle and repair plug material about two-thirds of the way into the hole. Pull the needle straight out and cut off any excess repair plug flush with the tire tread. Then reinflate the tire.

Tire Sealant

With ATVs, the best policy is to prevent a flat in the first place. Applying a tire sealant before you use the tire can prevent a lot of frustration. The MULTI-SEAL Corporation has a line of outdoor-sports-oriented tire sealants, including one specifically engineered for ATVs. The products come conveniently packaged in 32-ounce bottles with delivery tubes and valve wrenches attached to each package. One bottle per tire is recommended for ATVs. These corrosion-inhibiting formulations are completely compatible with tire and wheel materials, protect against punctures up to 0.25 inch deep,

Tire sealant can be a problem preventer if you ride in country with thorns or sharp rocks.

and are guaranteed for the life of the tire. They use a complex blend of multisized fibers and fillers in a robust liquid suspension system. All MULTI-SEAL products are corrosion inhibited for steel, aluminum, and yellow metals used in rims and valve parts.

Installation of MULTI-SEAL is easy. Rotate the tire until the valve stem is at the 12 o'clock position, then remove the valve core from the stem with the tool included in the package. Cut off the tip of the bottle, attach a hose to the tip, and place the end of the hose over the valve stem. Then pump the formulation into the tire to a specified volume (one bottle per tire for ATVs) by simply holding up and squeezing the bottle. Replace the valve core and reinflate the tire to its recommended air pressure. Do not overinflate the tires. The material is water soluble and washes quickly and easily from your hands, the tire, and the rim. The country I hunt is ideal for testing the tire sealant formulation. Hedge trees, locust thorns, and sharp Ozark rocks have in the past necessitated frequent tire repairs and caused numerous headaches. With the formulation in my ATV tires, however, I've had no problems.

The type of riding you do will determine to a great extent the amount and types of servicing needed. If you operate frequently in mud, dust, or other harsh riding conditions, you'll need more frequent servicing.

Although you can do a great deal of maintenance yourself, some operations must be performed by a dealer to ensure your warranty. This is explained in your owner's manual.

Don't neglect the maintenance of your ATV. Modern ATVs are very sophisticated, true, but they're also easier to maintain. With proper maintenance, they can provide many years of service.

Sources

MANUFACTURERS

API Outdoors, 800-228-4846, www.apioutdoors.com

All Rite Products, Inc., 800-771-8471, www.allriteproducts.com

Arctic Cat, 800-3-ARCTIC, www.arcticcat.com

Argo, 519-662-4000, www.argoatv.com

Avery Outdoors, Inc., 800-333-5119, www.averyoutdoors.com

Bad Boy Buggies, 866-678-6701, www.badboybuggies.com

BASF, 800-545-9525, www.basf.com, www.vmanswers.com

Bass Pro Shops, 800-BASS PRO, www.basspro.com

Bobcat, 701-241-8700, www.bobcat.com

Bombardier, 877-469-7433, www.bombardier-atv.com

Brewer Implement Company, 229-387-7888, www.
    sportsmenoutdoors.com

CDS, Inc., 800-791-1333, www.cdsatvaccessories.com

Cabela's, 800-237-4444, www.cabelas.com

Club Car, 800-258-2227, www.ClubCar.com

Cub Cadet, www.cubcadet.com

Cycle Country, 800-841-2222, www.cyclecountry.com

Deere & Company, 309-765-8000, www.deere.com

Essex Manufacturing Company, 888-64-ESSEX, www.essexmfg.com

E-Z-GO, 800-241-5855, www.EZGO.com

Gun Vault, 800-222-1055, www.gunvault.com

High Lifter Products, Inc., 318-524-2270, www.highlifter.com

Hi-Per Sports, Inc., 800-241-2222, www.hipersports.com

Honda, 310-783-3743, www.honda.com

ICC, a division of Wallingford's Inc., 207-465-9575, www.
    wallingfords.com

ITP, Industrial Tire Products, Inc., 909-390-1905, www.itptires.com

Kawasaki, 800-661-RIDE, www.kawasaki.com

Kolpin Manufacturing, Inc., 877-956-5746, www.kolpin.com
Kubota, www.kubota.com
Louisiana Guard Dog, T & W Manufacturing, LLC, 800-809-4118,
   www.laguarddog.com
Mad Dog Gear, 800-333-1179, www.stearnsinc.com
Masterbuilt Manufacturing Company, 800-489-1581, www.
   masterbuilt.com
Mossy Oak BioLogic, 888-MOSSY-OAK
Moultrie Feeders, 800-653-3334, www.moultriefeeders.com
MULTI-SEAL Corporation, 800-577-3353, www.multi-seal.com
Northern Tool & Equipment Company, 800-533-5545, www.
   northern-online.com
NovaJack, 800-567-7318, www.novajack.com
Original DeerLift, 800-738-LIFT, www.deerlift.com
Otter Outdoors, 877-GO-OTTER, www.otteroutdoors.com
OxLite Manufacturing, 800-256-2408, www.oxlite.com
Pa-Paw's ATV Game Hoist, 888-4PA-PAWS
Plano Molding, 800-226-9868, www.planomolding.com
Plotmaster, Tecomate Wildlife Systems, 888-MAX-GAME, www.
   theplotmaster.com
Polaris, 800-POLARIS, www.polarisindustries.com
Quadivator, Swisher, Inc., 800-222-8183, www.swisherinc.com
Recreative Industries, 800-255-2511, www.maxatvs.com
Rugged Gear, 800-784-4331, www.ruggedgear.com
Rule Industries, Inc., 978-281-0440, www.rule-industries.com
SuperWinch, 860-928-7787, www.superwinch.com
Suzuki, 800-828-RIDE, www.suzukicycles.com
Tamarack, LaBoite, Inc., 800-269-6701, www.tamarackatv.com
Tarter Gate Company, 800-733-4283, www.tartergate.com
Triton Trailers, 800-232-3780, www.tritontrailers.com
Tufline, 662-328-8347, www.monroetufline.com
Walk-Winn Co., 800-362-9154
Warn Industries, 800-543-WARN, www.warnindustries.com
Weekend Warrior, 866-539-8944, www.weekend-warrior.com
Yamaha, 800-88-YAMAHA, www.yamaha.com

ORGANIZATIONS AND INFORMATION

ATV Safety Institute (ASI), 949-727-3727, www.atvsafety.org
ATV RiderCourse, 800-887-2887, www.atvsafety.org

Americans for Responsible Recreational Access, www.
   responsiblerecreation.org
Consumer Product Safety Commission, 800-638-2772,
   www.cpsc.gov
Grand National Cross Country, 304-284-0084, www.gnccracing.com
National 4-H Council, 7100 Connecticut Avenue, Chevy Chase, MD
   20815, www.4-H.org
National Off-Highway Vehicle Conservation Council, 800-348-6487,
   www.nohvcc.org
Paiute ATV Trail System, www.atvutah.com
Parents, Youngsters and ATVs, ASI, 800-887-2887
Specialty Vehicle Institute of America (SVIA), 949-727-3727,
   www.svia.org
Tread Lightly!, 800-966-9900, www.treadlightly.org

Glossary

air filter A user-serviceable part that supplies clean air to the engine.

boot protector Protects the rubber CV boots on the front-wheel driveshaft.

CC Stands for "cubic centimeters" and describes the size of the engine.

CV boots Rubber boots that protect the front-wheel driveshaft.

center articulation An ATV with independent front and rear.

centrifugal clutch Applies a specific amount of pressure on the drive belt according to the centrifugal force.

chain-drive transmission An ATV transmission utilizing chains and sprockets.

differential An axle that permits independent drive of each wheel.

dual-mode differential A differential that can be locked or unlocked.

engine braking The use of engine compression and torque to slow the ATV.

footboards The platform on the ATV to place your feet.

footpegs Pegs on ATV to place your feet, in addition to footboards.

free-wheeling An ATV without engine-braking capabilities. Manual braking must be applied to slow the machine.

gear drive transmission An ATV transmission featuring a fully enclosed gear drive.

independent rear suspension A suspension system utilizing two shocks.

off-highway or **off-road vehicle** Any vehicle, including off-highway motorcycles and ATVs, that is restricted by law from operating on public roads.

parking brake A mechanism that holds the brake in the on position.

payload The amount of weight that can be carried.

psi Refers to air pressure in the tires and stands for "pounds per square inch."

powertrain The combination of engine and transmission.

rack capacity The amount of weight the rack will carry as specified by the manufacturer.

recoil starter The pull cord mechanism used to start some ATV engines.

reading the terrain Looking well ahead while riding, anticipating hazards.

receiver hitch A slide-in front or rear hitch.

RPM Stands for "revolutions per minute" and is used to describe the engine speed.

selectable drive An ATV capable of switching between two- and four-wheel drive.

shift On ATVs equipped with a shift lever, it allows the operator to change gears.

shift-on-the-fly Ability to shift between two- and four-wheel drive while the ATV is moving.

sidehilling Driving an ATV sideways across the slope of a hill.

6WD A six-wheel-drive system.

skid plate A plate that protects the bottom of the ATV.

snorkel air intake A system that brings clean, fresh air into the engine.

spark arrestor A necessary piece of equipment that prevents sparks from escaping the exhaust system.

spark plug A user-serviceable part within the engine that provides the spark for ignition.

sport model An ATV used for off-road recreation.

swingarm That portion of the ATV suspension that holds the shock absorbers.

swingarm rear suspension A suspension that utilizes two shocks.

switchback A sharp curve on a trail that is used to change direction, usually on steep hillsides.

tailpipe That part of the exhaust system that expels waste gases.

throttle The control operated by the right hand or thumb that controls the engine speed.

throttle limiter A governor that controls engine speed.

torque converter Provides for engine braking.

towing capacity The amount of weight an ATV can tow as specified by the manufacturer.

traction Tread friction between the ground and the tires.

tripmeter An ATV mileage log.

transmission The series of gears, shafts, belts, chains, and sprockets used to transmit power from the engine to the wheels.

12-volt plug An accessory plug for cell phone, lights, and so forth.

utility/cargo ATVs ATVs with dual person/cargo capabilities.

utility ATVs ATVs used for both recreation and work.

weight transfer A change in rider weight distribution to control an ATV while maneuvering.

Index

Note: Page numbers in italics indicate photos.